Thinking Organized

For Parents and Children

WORKBOOK

Helping Kids Get ORGANIZED for Home, School and Play

Rhona M. Gordon, M.S., CCC/SLP

Thinking ORGANIZED

Silver Spring, MD

Thinking Organized™ for Parents and Children Workbook: Helping Kids Get Organized for Home, School, and Play by Rhona M. Gordon, M.S., CCC/SLP

Published by Thinking Organized Press,
8639-B Sixteenth Street, Ste. 290, Silver Spring, MD 20910.
Visit www.ThinkingOrganized.com for more information.

Cover photos courtesy of Corbis Images

ISBN–13: 978-0-9790034-5-5
ISBN–10: 0-9790034-5-8

Printed in the United States of America
12 11 10 09 08 07   6   5   4   3   2   1

Contents

Why Develop Executive Functioning Skills? 5

How to Use the Thinking Organized Workbook 7

Available at ThinkingOrganized.com 11

Strategy 1: Material Organization 13

Strategy 2: Time Management 23

Strategy 3: Learning Styles and Studying 39

Strategy 4: MemoryStrategies 53

Strategy 5: Note-Taking to Improve Reading Comprehension 85

Strategy 6: Written Language Skills 95

Glossary 123

Bibliography 125

About the Author 126

User Removable Worksheets 127

A Note to the Reader:

Thank you for purchasing the *Thinking Organized Workbook*. This workbook has been designed to provide you with the hands-on tools to teach your child the strategies presented in *Thinking Organized for Parents and Children: Helping Kids Get Organized for Home, School, and Play*. We hope this workbook will be a big time-saver for you in improving your child's executive functioning skills.

In my practice, I work with many children. I want to represent both boys and girls in this book and therefore have chosen to alternate the use of masculine and feminine pronouns by chapter. The examples that I use in the book are real; however, the names are completely fictitious and chosen at random.

Why Develop Executive Functioning Skills?

Steven loses his homework in his own backpack.
Ellen comes home in thirty-degree weather without her coat.
Billy procrastinates until he is forced to pull an all-nighter.
Stacy spends hours studying but still gets bad test grades.
John freaks out when he has to write anything, from a paragraph
to a research paper.

It's a fact of life that some students, even those who are very bright, just can't seem to get it together. Lost items, forgotten paperwork, and last-minute requests cause chaos for the whole family. Sometimes these children have trouble preparing for exams, keeping information in memory, and expressing their thoughts clearly and precisely in writing. Many professionals have labeled this group of difficulties as executive functioning weaknesses. Executive functions are defined as the mental organizational processes by which a person can plan and sequence ideas or activities and then implement, monitor, and revise these activities as needed. This process is not only necessary for children managing their schoolwork but it is essential in every aspect of adult life. For example, a mother with poor executive functioning skills may plan a party and underestimate the amount of food needed, forget to pick up the cake, or scramble around at the last minute to pull everything together. If something changes (like bad weather or burned food), she has a difficult time adjusting her plans to compensate.

In school, executive functioning skills form the underlying basis for successful academic achievement. From simple tasks such as managing supplies to more complex ones such as writing a research paper, the ability to plan, monitor, revise, and complete an activity is crucial. Adults working in a job are required to learn and repeat skills that are similar from day to day. Children must remember many different facts from a variety of disciplines, even those that hold no interest for them personally. Not only are students required to learn and memorize large chunks of material, but they are also expected to form ideas and concepts from that material and present it in an organized format—a tall order for a disorganized thinker.

However, there are ways that a parent can help a child with these kinds of problems, systems that can be put in place to make each day run more smoothly and teach a child to manage her own time and materials. The *Thinking Organized*™ program has been developed over years of working with students of varying ages and abilities. The program addresses those areas that are consistently more difficult for the disorganized student. This workbook will give you the hands-on tools needed to learn and practice the six aspects of effective executive functioning skills: material organization, time management, studying strategies, memory techniques, note-taking for reading comprehension, and written language. Students who have completed the program, as well as their parents, have reported that *Thinking Organized*™ is the only program that seems to address *all* their areas of weakness. By teaching these strategies to your child, you are taking the first step to helping your child establish executive functioning skills that will be used throughout her life.

How to Use the
Thinking Organized Workbook

efore working with your child, review the preparation page in this workbook and gather the necessary supplies. Each strategy has a set of goals that the student should work toward during the coming week. Explain the goals and use the checklist to work through each strategy step by step. At the end of the session, review the skills you have practiced and explain what is required of your student during the week ahead.

Be sure to plan a consistent time to introduce each new strategy. Some parents schedule one strategy each week; others find their child needs more time to practice. Establish your own routine, but plan to meet with your child the same time every week. Do not leave the timing to chance or plan on "sometime this weekend." It is important to establish a day and time for learning and reviewing *Thinking Organized*™ strategies. Maintaining a consistent schedule not only helps the child learn a routine, but it also helps secure the time in the parent's busy week.

After introducing a new strategy to your child, it is important to reinforce it daily. For example, the assignment notebook should be checked every single school day (a goal of Strategy One, Material Organization). Many skills are also easy for a parent to reinforce on a more informal basis. A few minutes stuck in the car or trapped in a waiting room can be well spent by playing a memory game (Strategy Four) or discussing a current event to foster critical thinking (Strategy Six).

Work through the strategies at your own pace. Children with organizational difficulties are not all the same. One student may have considerable trouble with time management but little trouble maintaining her materials. For this child, the parent may want to review quickly the first strategy on Material Organization but spend more time teaching the strategies on Time Management. The parent is the best judge of the skills that need the most attention. Plan to spend most of your time practicing the strategies that address your child's specific areas of weakness.

Achieving a Balance in Motivating Your Child

*I*t is difficult to change familiar habits, and sometimes students feel that taking an extra step to get organized is a waste of time. In the beginning, your child may resist the *Thinking Organized*™ program, but after practicing on a continuous basis, the strategies will become routine. At this point, your child will truly believe for herself that these systems of organization will save her time and improve her grades.

So is it better to motivate children by withholding privileges, for example, "If you don't file your papers you don't get to watch TV?" Or is the promise of a reward a better way to get results, by giving incentives when students perform as desired? We have found that most students genuinely want to do well in school and please their parents and teachers, and therefore, rewarding positive behavior is the most effective tool to help your child develop new skills for managing life.

For older and more resistant children, a combination approach of positive reinforcements and consequences may work better. For example, if a child frequently forgets to turn in homework, a parent could reward the child when she does turn in her work, and take away a privilege (such as TV, video games, or, for an older student, the use of the car) when the goal is not met.

Decide on what type of reward system will work best for your child. Each week, be sure to explain exactly what is expected and what reward she is working toward. Here are some suggestions:

- We strongly recommend the use of charts. They are an excellent visual reminder of the student's progress. The *Thinking Organized*™ charts provided in this workbook detail each specific goal to help the student remember exactly what is expected. A star or a checkmark for each day the student correctly meets each goal could add up to a reward or privilege at the end of the week.

- Activity rewards can represent extra privileges, such as picking a favorite board game, going to the playground, or playing games on the computer.

- Tangible rewards, such as small toys or treats, should be used in moderation to remain effective. One idea is to give the child collectible rewards such as baseball or trading cards, doll clothes, or coins from other countries. Alternatively, the reward can have several parts to be given over time, for example, parts of a model airplane or Lego® kit.

- An older student is more likely to be motivated by something she can choose herself, such as a gift certificate for a video rental, fast food, or a clothing store. When the student completes a goal, she can earn points to be applied toward the gift certificate.

Communication is an important part of the process. Be quick to praise your student for her efforts. Verbal praise and recognition are important reinforcements that encourage the child to keep trying. When she encounters failure, show her how to correct the mistake and move on.

Many parents believe that proper motivation is the key to the successful implementation of the *Thinking Organized*™ program. However, the student will see her grades improve, her day to day life run smoother, and that she is able to read, study, and write more effectively. This will gradually motivate her to continue the strategies on her own. You will naturally phase out the reward program as the strategies become habit. However, it is helpful to continue to occasionally reward adherence to the underlying skills that are contributing to her success. Everyone likes their efforts to be noticed and appreciated!

Available at ThinkingOrganized.com

- **Supplies:** Many of the supplies you will need to help your child start "thinking organized" are available on our website, www.ThinkingOrganized.com. Multi-color pens, customized notebooks, binders, and study kits are among the many items you will find online.

- **Seminars:** A seminar is a fantastic way to share knowledge and expenses among many interested individuals. Our seminars have been customized for professional groups, educators, parents and students. Check out what others have to say and the variety of topics available at www.ThinkingOrganized.com.

- **Distance Consultations:** Now you can schedule a block of time as small as one half-hour with one of our staff members to discuss specific difficulties you're experiencing with managing your time, organizing your daily life or keeping a student on track. Not just an organizational coach, Thinking Organized professionals use the study of the brain and language to develop new solutions for persistent problems.

- **Monthly Tips:** Each month a Thinking Organized tip is emailed to our growing list of educators, parents and students who want to improve their knowledge of executive functioning skills. Visit www.ThinkingOrganized.com to join our mailing list and receive monthly tips and advance notice of new material.

Strategy One

Material Organization

*M*aterial organization is the first strategy introduced in the *Thinking Organized*™ program, because students need an effective system to keep track of assignments and paperwork. This is a baseline skill in the organizational process. It is very difficult to do well in school if a student is missing homework sheets, assignments, or study guides or if he lacks a clear system for documenting and monitoring his assignments.

It is important for the student to use the structures introduced in this chapter every day in order for the skills to become routinized. Even if your child does not like the system, during the training period you must insist on daily adherence in order to establish effective material organization.

GOALS

1. **Assignment notebook:** Set up an assignment notebook and learn how to use it to document work. Plan to check the notebook after school each day and devote time to improving entries.

2. **Binder:** The student will develop and maintain a system to keep papers neatly organized.

3. **Other materials:** A dedicated area will be established for items needed every day such as a student's coat, keys, cell phone, or backpack.

WORKSHEETS

Worksheet One: **An Assignment Notebook Ready for Use.**
This worksheet will be a guide to help you set up an assignment notebook tailored to your student. You will list each class and include a row for extracurricular activities and a "Don't Forget" section. A user removable worksheet is available on page 129 of the user worksheet section.

Worksheet Two: **Sample Completed Assignment Notebook.**
This worksheet will help you explain to your student the method of listing homework during the day, the use of the "Don't Forget" section, and the check/ cross-check boxes.

Worksheet Three: **Assignment Notebook Rules.**

Tape these rules to the inside front cover of the assignment notebook. These will help your student properly complete the assignment notebook every day. A user removable worksheet is available on page 131 of the user worksheet section.

Worksheet Four: **Reward Chart.**

Use this chart to keep track of your student's progress in implementing Strategy One. User removable worksheets are available on page 133 and 134 of the user worksheet section.

PREPARATION

1. Purchase an assignment notebook. Frequently schools have their own assignment notebooks that the students must use. If not, then choose a notebook with wide spaces for entries and margins for notes.

2. Have on hand a multi-colored pen to help the child color-code his notebook.

3. Purchase one of the following systems to maintain the student's papers.

    a. Some teachers require that the student use a three-ring binder. If so, provide one two-pocket folder for each subject to help with papers that are not hole-punched.

    b. Older students sometimes prefer to use an accordion folder. If so, purchase a six- or twelve-pocket folder and labels.

    c. If the student chooses to have a separate notebook for each subject, be sure to choose notebooks with pocket folders to help him keep papers neat.

4. Prepare an area in the house for other materials. Establish an area for your child to put everyday things such as his keys, cell phone, and backpack. This will become the first place he stops when arriving home and the last stop before leaving the house again.

Strategy One

Material Organization Checklist

Set Up Assignment Notebook

❏ 1. Write subjects and dates for one month. Do not include subjects that rarely give homework (i.e., chorus or P.E.).

❏ 2. Make a section for extracurricular activities, such as sports, clubs, religious school, or chores.

❏ 3. Make a "Don't Forget" section to list supplies needed for homework, like textbooks.

❏ 4. Color code all information:
　　　　Red = Test or Quiz
　　　　Blue = Long-term Project
　　　　Black = Nightly Homework
　　　　Green = Fun Activities

❏ 5. Create and use a check/cross-check box.
　　　　☑ Check when the assignment is finished.
　　　　☒ Cross-check when the assignment is placed in
　　　　　 the binder and put into the backpack.

❏ 6. Complete every box every day. Ask teachers to sign the assignment notebook. An older student will need to have it signed after each class, whereas the younger student with one teacher can have the assignment notebook signed at the end of the day. Parents should sign the assignment notebook when all homework is completed and packed in the backpack.

Set Up Binder

Choose and set up a binder:

❏ 1. **Traditional three-ring:** Add folder pockets and supply pouch.

❏ 2. **Accordion File:** Customize the folder for your student. One way to organize the accordion folder is to leave the front pocket for current homework, the second section for the assignment notebook, and the back pocket for blank paper. Label the remaining pockets in the order of your child's classes, and file papers so the most current ones are in the front.

❏ 3. **Separate notebooks for each subject:** Be sure folder pockets are included.

Check and reorganize daily if needed.

❏   Other Materials

Help the student develop a well-stocked, dedicated area for homework and a separate area for things needed each day (jacket, cell phone, and wallet).

Strategy One

Assignment Notebook

Strategy One, User Worksheet One

A user removable worksheet is available on page 129 of the user worksheet section.

Subject	Monday __/__	Tuesday __/__	Wednesday __/__	Thursday __/__	Friday __/__	Saturday __/__	Sunday __/__
___	☐	☐	☐	☐	☐	☐	☐
___	☐	☐	☐	☐	☐	☐	☐
___	☐	☐	☐	☐	☐	☐	☐
___	☐	☐	☐	☐	☐	☐	☐
___	☐	☐	☐	☐	☐	☐	☐
___	☐	☐	☐	☐	☐	☐	☐
Don't Forget							
Extra Curricular							
Teacher's Signature							
Parent's Signature							

Strategy One, User Worksheet Two

Sample Assignment Notebook

	Monday 12/3	Tuesday 12/4	Wednesday 12/5	Thursday 12/6	Friday 12/7	Saturday 12/8	Sunday 12/9
Math	P. 127 – even only. Re-read text of chapter 3 for test [X]	P. 127 – odd only. Redo all missed questions from chapter 3 homework [X]	Take end of chapter test [X]	FINAL REVIEW. Reread chap. 3 and rework hardest problems [X]	Chap. 3 Test. Homework: read intro to chap. 4 [X]	2 PM – do math reading [X]	[ ]
English	None [ ]	Make index cards of poetry terms [X]	Date with Mom to cal out poetry terms [X]	Final review of poetry terms [X]	Poetry test. No homework [X]	12:30 – Go to library to get book for report [X]	[ ]
Science	Read chapter 2, pages 15 - 20 [X]	Chap 2 pages 21-30. Research 3 different types of butterflies for project [X]	List out features of 3 butterflies. Start drawing pictures [X]	Finish drawings and check project for grammar/spelling [X]	Butterfly project due. Homework: read pages 41-50 in chap. 3 [X]	2 PM – science reading [X]	[ ]
Spanish	Date with Mom to shop for ingredients [X]	Make enchiladas tonight [X]	SPANISH FOOD PROJECT DUE [X]	None [ ]	None [ ]	[ ]	2:30: review vocabulary list from last week [X]
Geography	Get blank maps for practice – make cards for capitals [X]	Practice filling in map. Make up memory tricks [X]	Have Mom practice with capital cards – recite memory tricks for Mom [X]	Review all cards and practice filling in map [X]	Asia TEST. No homework [X]	[ ]	[ ]
Don't Forget	Math book and science book	Math book and science book	Math book, science book and HOCKEY GEAR	Poetry handouts, geography book and math book	Math book and science book. Bring CD for Grandpa	Get/make cookies for Youth Group	Pack book for report. Math and science books
Extra Curricular			Michael comes over after school!!	Hockey practice	Dinner with grandparents	Hockey game at 10:00 AM	Youth Group at 7:00 PM
Teacher's Signature	Mrs. Smith	Mrs. Smith	Mrs. Smith	Mrs. Smith	Mrs. Smith		
Parent's Signature	Mr. John Doe	Mr. John Doe	Mr. John Doe	Mr. John Doe	Mr. John Doe		

©2008, Rhona M. Gordon. Thinking Organized™. All Rights Reserved. Duplication permitted by owner of *Thinking Organized for Parents and Children Workbook*

Strategy One

Strategy One, User Worksheet Three

Assignment Notebook Rules

A user removable worksheet is available on page 131 of the user worksheet section.

Tape this page to the inside of the assignment notebook.

1. Create a "Don't Forget" section for each week when you label your subjects for the month.

2. Color code all information:
   Red = Test or Quiz
   Blue = Long-term Project
   Black = Nightly Homework
   Green = Fun

3. Complete every box every day.
   If there is no homework, write "NONE" in the box.

4. Make a section for extracurricular activities, including tutoring, sports, clubs, or religious school.

5. Create and use a check/cross-check box.
   ☑ Check when assignment is completed.
   ☒ Cross-check when assignment is packed in binder.

Ask Mom or Dad to sign the assignment notebook every night.
He or she can only sign when Steps 1–5 have been completed.

Homework

Strategy One, User Worksheet Four

User removable worksheets are available on page 133 and 134 of the user worksheet section.
Maintain a properly organized assignment notebook and binder system. Remember to use the check in/check out location when arriving or leaving home. Points can be awarded for each day that the systems are used correctly.

Reward Chart

		Monday	Tuesday	Wednesday	Thursday	Friday	Saturday	Sunday
Assignment Notebook	Color coding							
	"Don't Forget" section							
	Writing something in every subject							
	Check/cross check							
Binder	Papers filed							
	Pockets used							
Other	Daily check in/out							

Strategy One

Strategy One

BEFORE MOVING ON . . .

Material organization is a *big* stumbling block for many students and a skill that needs daily attention. Many parents begin by going through the student's backpack every day after school, ensuring that papers are filed properly and work is organized neatly. When the student begins to adopt these strategies independently, a weekly monitoring may be all that is needed. Regardless, the assignment notebook must be checked daily until the student is completely accurate in documenting homework.

Strategy Two

Time
Management

*T*ime management is one of life's most important skills, and it often causes great difficulty for children as well as adults. Missed appointments, consistent tardiness, and a feeling of being constantly rushed are among the frustrations caused by the inability to manage one's time.

As a student becomes conscious of time, it is easier for her to succeed in school and extracurricular activities. A student with executive function weaknesses frequently has difficulty managing time effectively. She may have trouble estimating how long an assignment will take and therefore experience frustration when she leaves too little time to complete a project. When given a task with multiple steps, such as a research paper, the student may struggle to break the project down into manageable parts.

Fortunately, time-management skills can be learned. Parents can help students become aware of time every day: how it is spent, how it is wasted, how it is planned, and how quickly it passes. Practicing the activities in this chapter—documenting time, estimating time, and breaking down long-term projects—will help your student become a better manager of her time and will ultimately benefit the whole family.

GOALS

1. **Awareness:** Increase the student's awareness of time by using time logs and encouraging your student to wear and look at her watch.

2. **Estimation:** Improve the student's ability to estimate time by using the guess/actual time sheets.

3. **Scheduling long-term projects:** Teach the student how to break long-term projects into specific tasks and schedule each one appropriately.

WORKSHEETS

Worksheet One: **Sample Time Log.** First, block out the amount of time that is already accounted for, such as for school or other obligations. This gives an instant visual display of how much time is actually *not* available for homework or projects. The student can then list how the remaining time was spent each day.

Worksheet Two: **Blank Time Log.** Several copies of the time log have been provided for you to practice this skill with your child. User removable worksheets are available beginning on page 135 of the user worksheet section.

Worksheet Three: **Sample Guess/Actual Time Sheet for Going to Bed.** The sample will give you an idea of how to complete the guess/actual time sheet for a daily activity such as getting ready for bed.

Worksheet Four: **Sample Guess/Actual Time Sheet for Homework.** This sample will give you an idea of how to complete the guess/actual time sheet for one night of homework.

Worksheet Five: **Blank Guess/Actual Time Sheet.** Keep these on hand and practice guessing how long an activity will take, then recording the actual time spent. As your student gets better at this skill, she can record her guess/actual times right in the assignment notebook. Several user removable worksheets are available beginning on page 141 of the user worksheet section.

Worksheet Six: **Sample Activities for Practicing Guess/Actual Timing.** These activities will give you ideas for more ways to practice estimating time.

Worksheet Seven: **Sample Activities for Practicing Your Family's Guess/Actual Timing.** This worksheet is a list of family activities that can be used to practice estimating time.

Worksheet Eight: **Sample Monthly Calendar with Planned Project.** This sample will be a guide in helping you demonstrate the steps of breaking a long-term project into specific and meaningful tasks.

Worksheet Nine: **Sample Monthly Calendar.** This calendar demonstrates the color-coding system and an effective way to set up a calendar for either your student or the whole family.

Worksheet Ten: **Blank Monthly Calendar.** This can be used for practice with breaking down long-term projects. User removable worksheets are available beginning on page 149 of the user worksheet section.

Worksheet Eleven: **Homework and Reward Chart.** Post the chart in a prominent place, such as on the refrigerator, so points can be rewarded each time one of the strategies is used. A user removable worksheet is available on page 151 of the user worksheet section.

PREPARATION

1. You will need the following supplies:

   A watch for your child

   Kitchen timer

   Multi-colored pen

   Time logs and guess/actual time sheet

   Blank monthly calendar

2. Collect information about your family's monthly plans and your child's extracurricular activities in order to add these to a family monthly calendar.

3. Gather information about upcoming homework and assignments, either online or by using the student's assignment notebook. These can be added to the monthly calendar or used for practice in dividing lengthy assignments.

Strategy Two

Time Management Checklist

The checklist is a guide to help you progress through each step of teaching time management to your child.

☐ 1. Use the time log to demonstrate how time is scheduled, spent and wasted. First, use a highlighter to box off all of the time that is already accounted for, such as time spent in school or sports practice. Next, have your student list how the remaining time is spent during each day, and discuss if time was used effectively.

☐ 2. Use the guess/actual time sheets to practice estimating time. These can be used frequently throughout the week when completing homework and other family activities.

☐ 3. Wear a watch. Be sure to give positive reinforcements when you see your child wearing a watch, and frequently remind her to check the time. For example, ask her what time it is now and how long until she needs to get ready for the next activity.

☐ 4. Demonstrate how long-term projects can be broken down into manageable parts, and list exact tasks in the assignment notebook or on a monthly calendar.

☐ 5. Practice completing a monthly calendar with the color patterns used in the assignment notebook:
      Red = Test or Quiz
      Blue = Long-term Project
      Black = Nightly Homework
      Green = Fun

Strategy Two

Sample Time Log

Strategy Two, Worksheet One
How Do I Spend My Time? Week of ___/___/___ to ___/___/___

Time	Monday __/__	Tuesday __/__	Wednesday __/__	Thursday __/__	Friday __/__	Saturday __/__	Sunday __/__
7:00 AM	Getting Ready for School – Shower, etc. →	→	→	→	→	Slept	Slept
8:00 AM	School	School	School	School	School	Slept	Shower
9:00 AM	→	→	→	→	→	Soccer	Religious School
10:00 AM	→	→	→	→	→	→	→
11:00 AM	→	→	→	→	→	→	→
12:00 PM	→	→	→	→	→	Shower	Lunch
1:00 PM	→	→	→	→	→	Lunch with Grandma	Cleaned my room
2:00 PM	→	→	→	→	→		Played computer
3:00 PM	→	→	→	→	→	Played video	Played with sister
4:00 PM	Played video	Soccer	Josh's House	Soccer	Josh Here	Took a nap	Homework
5:00 PM		Shower		Dinner at restaurant	→	Dinner	Hung out
6:00 PM	Dinner	Dinner	Dinner		Movies	Got ready for sleepover	Homework
7:00 PM	Walked dog	Homework	Hung out with Mom	Shower		Sleepover	Dinner
8:00 PM	Homework	Read my book	Homework	Homework	Played Video		Read my book
9:00 PM	Cleaned my room	Bed	Bed	Video Games			Played video
10:00 PM	Bed	→	→	Bed	Bed		Bed
11:00 PM	→	→	→	→	→		→
12:00 AM	→	→	→	→	→	Bed	→

Strategy Two, Worksheet Two

A user removable worksheet is available on page 135 of the user worksheet section.

How Do I Spend My Time? Week of ___/___/___ to ___/___/___

Time	Monday __/__	Tuesday __/__	Wednesday __/__	Thursday __/__	Friday __/__	Saturday __/__	Sunday __/__
7:00 AM							
8:00 AM							
9:00 AM							
10:00 AM							
11:00 AM							
12:00 PM							
1:00 PM							
2:00 PM							
3:00 PM							
4:00 PM							
5:00 PM							
6:00 PM							
7:00 PM							
8:00 PM							
9:00 PM							
10:00 PM							
11:00 PM							
12:00 AM							

Strategy Two

Strategy Two, Worksheet Three

Sample Guess/Actual Sheet for Going to Bed

Activity	Guess Time to Complete	Actual Time to Complete
Get backpack ready for tomorrow	5 min.	10 min. (couldn't find any pencils)
Get clothes ready for tomorrow	5 min.	15 min. (forgot to tell Mom to wash my gym clothes)
Take shower, brush teeth, wash face, and get into pajamas	30 min.	45 min.
Reading in bed	60 min.	45 min.

NOTES:

I like to read an hour in bed before I fall asleep, but because it took me longer than I thought to do everything else, I only had forty-five minutes to read. Tomorrow, I'll start earlier so I have more time to read.

Strategy Two, Worksheet Four

Sample Guess/Actual Sheet for Homework

Prioritize	Homework/Activity	Guess Time to Complete	Actual Time to Complete
2	Math sheet	15 minutes	25 minutes
1	Review notes for science test	60 minutes	30 minutes
3	Spanish verb sheet	20 minutes	40 minutes
4	Read novel	30 minutes	30 minutes

NOTES:

I knew the science material better than I thought, but both the worksheets took longer than expected.

Strategy Two, Worksheet Five

Guess/Actual Time Sheet

User removable worksheets are available beginning on page 141 of the user worksheet section.

Prioritize	Homework/Activity	Guess Time to Complete	Actual Time to Complete

NOTES

Strategy Two

Strategy Two, Worksheet Six

Sample Activities for Practicing Student's Guess/Actual Times

1. Going to sports practice

- How much time do you need to put your sports clothing on and get your equipment together?
- How long does it take to drive to practice?
- How much time is spent at practice?
- How long does it take to get home?
- What do you do when you get home? Shower? Put away gear? Relax? How much time is spent with these activities?

2. Play date with a friend

- How long does it take to organize the time and place?
- How much time is spent preparing activities for the play date?
- How long is spent on the actual play date?
- How much time is spent after the play date cleaning up, etc.?

3. Getting ready for bed

- How much time do you need to prepare your backpack and clothes for the next day?
- How long will it take you to shower, brush your teeth, and comb hair?
- How much time will be available for reading stories or other bedtime activities?

Strategy Two, Worksheet Seven

Sample Activites to Practice Your Family's Guess/Actual Times

1. Dinner

- How long does it take to prepare and serve dinner, even if you are not the one doing it? Include setting the table, getting everyone a drink, and serving the food.
- How much time does it take to eat dinner?
- How long does it take to clean up after dinner?

2. The family vacation

- How much time is spent choosing a place and picking the activities?
- How much time does it take to get the clothing together, pack medicines, music, books, etc.?
- How long is spent preparing the house (making arrangements for pets, mail, and work)?
- What is the travel time to and from destination?
- How long is spent after the trip: unpacking, putting away souvenirs, giving travel gifts, going through mail, e-mail, etc.?

Strategy Two, Worksheet Eight

Strategy Two

Sample Monthly Calendar with Planned Project

NOVEMBER

Sunday	Monday	Tuesday	Wednesday	Thursday	Friday	Saturday
	1 Topic chosen	2	3 Start research	4	5 Go to Library	6
7 Have research finished	8	9	10	11	12 Have notes organized	13
14	15 Have outline or Web completed	16	17 Start writing	18 Thanksgiving Relatives in town	19 NO SCHOOL Relatives in town	20
21	22	23 Finish writing	24 Peer review	24	26	27 Edit and revise
28 Final check	29	30 Research paper due				

Strategy Two, Worksheet Nine

RED = Tests or quizzes • BLACK = Nightly homework • BLUE = Long-term projects • Sample Monthly Calendar with Color Coding

however if you are using an assignment notebook it is not necessary to put homework on the long-term calendar • GREEN = Fun activities or weekly obligations

NOVEMBER

Sunday	Monday	Tuesday	Wednesday	Thursday	Friday	Saturday
	1 Research Project Choose Topic Math - page 42 English - worksheet	**2** Research Project Start Research Math - page 43 Science - worksheet	**3** Spanish Food Project Due Math - page 43-44	**4** Hockey Practice 8:00 - 9:00 p.m. 4 p.m. - Go to Library for Research Geography - Map	**5** Math Test Poetry Test Asia Test Butterfly Project	**6** Hockey Game 10:00 a.m.
7 Youth Group - 7 p.m. Research Project Have research finished	**8** Math - worksheet English - start chap. 2	**9** Math - page 50 English - worksheet	**10** ½ Day	**11** ½ Day Hockey Practice 8:00 - 9:00 p.m. Math - chapter 3 quiz	**12** Math Test Insect Project Research Project Notes Organized	**13** Family Trip to NY
14 Family Trip to NY	**15** Research Project Outline Completed Math - page 56 English - start chap. 3	**16** Hockey Game - 8 p.m. Math - review	**17** Research Project Start Writing Science - worksheet English - grammar	**18** THANKSGIVING Relatives in town	**19** No School Relatives in town	**20** Relatives in town
21 Relatives in town	**22** Science - worksheet English - grammar	**23** Hockey Game - 8 p.m. Math - page 61 English - start chap. 4	**24** Research Project Peer Check	**25** Hockey Practice 8:00 - 9:00 p.m. Spanish Poster Due Science - worksheet English - grammar	**26** Math Test Shakespeare Test	**27** Edit and Revise Hockey Game 3:00 p.m.
28 Research Project Final Check	**29**	**30** Research Project Due				

©2008, Rhona M. Gordon, Thinking Organized™. All Rights Reserved. Duplication permitted by owner of *Thinking Organized for Parents and Children Workbook*

Strategy Two

Strategy Two, Worksheet Ten

User removable worksheets are available beginning on page 149 of the user worksheet section.

RED = Tests or quizzes • BLUE = Long-term projects • BLACK = Nightly homework, however if you are using an assignment notebook it is not necessary to put homework on the long-term calendar • GREEN = Fun activities or weekly obligations

Strategy Two

Blank Monthly Calendar

Sunday	Monday	Tuesday	Wednesday	Thursday	Friday	Saturday

Homework

Strategy Two, Worksheet Eleven

A user removable worksheet is available on page 151 of the user worksheet section.

Throughout this week, help your child practice estimating, recording, and noticing time by using the time logs, guess/actual time sheets, the monthly calendar, and her watch. Remember to continue to give points for use of the assignment notebook and binder as introduced in Strategy One.

Reward Chart

		Monday	Tuesday	Wednesday	Thursday	Friday	Saturday	Sunday
Assignment Notebook	Color coding							
	"Don't Forget" section							
	Writing something in every subject							
	Check/cross check							
Binder	Papers filed							
	Pockets used							
Other	Daily check in/out							
Time Management	Time log							
	Guess/ actual time sheets							
	Wearing a watch							

Strategy Two

BEFORE MOVING ON . . .

Time management is an important life skill that will make every day less stressful and more productive. Frequent practice is necessary for most children to become aware of the passage of time and to become good estimators of how long a task will take. You can informally reinforce this skill by frequently noting the time, reminding your child to check her watch, and consulting your monthly calendar together. By teaching your child effective time-management strategies, you are helping her to make the most of every day. When her academic work and extra-curricular activities increase, she will have in place the strategies to effectively meet her deadlines and obligations.

Strategy Three

Learning Styles and Studying

*S*tudying is a skill that can be taught. Many of my students have noticed that better grades are not a result of spending more time studying but studying more effectively. Start by determining if your child prefers to learn by a primarily visual, auditory, or kinesthetic modality. Although most students learn visually, and some visual learning is necessary for every student, knowing if your student responds to auditory or kinesthetic methods can make studying much more effective. The visual learner relies mostly on his sense of sight, an auditory student learns mostly by listening and speaking, and a kinesthetic learner likes to touch things and move around. Using more than one learning style often helps students become better engaged with the material and facilitates the learning process.

Effective studying begins when the student first reads the material. Demonstrating active reading techniques such as previewing text, highlighting or note-taking, and jotting down questions will help the child retain more of the information he has read. Next, discuss the steps of studying for a test, including proper scheduling, study guides, and integrating information for essay questions.

GOALS

1. Help the student discover more about his individual learning style and preferences.

2. Incorporate some new studying techniques that will appeal to his style of learning and encourage his studying flexibility by trying strategies from different modalities. For example, if your student is a visual learner, have him try some auditory techniques.

3. Practice good studying habits every day to ensure that work is current and no materials are missing. Implement specific techniques to help a student study for a quiz or test.

WORKSHEETS

Worksheet One: **Learning Styles Assessment Questionnaire.** Read through each question with your child, and let him choose the answer that best describes him. This will help you determine if your student seems to prefer a visual, auditory, or kinesthetic learning style. A user removable worksheet is available on page 153 of the user worksheet section.

Worksheet Two: **Strategies for the Three Learning Modalities.** Encourage your student to try strategies that appeal to his primary learning style, as well as strategies from the other two modalities.

Worksheet Three: **Studying for a Test, On Your Mark . . .** If your student follows these guidelines, he'll know 80 percent of the material. A user removable worksheet is available on page 155 of the user worksheet section.

Worksheet Four: **Studying for a Test, Get Set . . .** This worksheet gives your student specific studying techniques to use when preparing for a test. A user removable worksheet is available on page 157 of the user worksheet section.

Worksheet Five: **Studying for a Test, Go!** The final steps to effectively prepare for any kind of test—essay or multiple choice. A user removable worksheet is available on page 159 of the user worksheet section.

Worksheet Six: **Memorizing Material.** This will give your student suggestions for memorizing material for a test or quiz. How to Memorize? A user removable worksheet is available on page 161 of the user worksheet section.

Worksheet Seven: **Homework and Reward Chart.** Have this available during the week to reward your child for trying new and different ways to study. A user removable worksheet is available on page 163 of the user worksheet section.

Strategy Three

PREPARATION

1. Have on hand a social studies or science textbook or any non-fiction text that is not too difficult for your child to read and understand. This will be helpful in demonstrating that studying begins when the student first reads text material.

2. Prepare a dedicated study area. You may decide to include gum, a water bottle, or a squishy ball as aids for focusing and maintaining concentration. Sometimes having a physical manipulative helps the student stay focused on his work rather than searching for a distraction in the environment.

3. Be prepared to offer new suggestions and supplies to increase your student's interaction with the material to be learned. Index cards, post-it notes, a CD or tape player, or even a new pack of colored pens can provide a fresh approach and renewed enthusiasm for studying.

Strategy Three

Learning Styles and Studying Checklist

The checklist is a guide to help you progress through each step of teaching learning styles and studying to your child.

❏ 1. Help the student begin to assess his own learning style by answering the questions on Worksheet One.

❏ 2. Encourage the student to try studying techniques that involve his preferred learning style, but also try strategies from the other two learning styles:

    Visual: Flash cards, diagrams, or outlines

    Auditory: Tapes, CDs, or oral recitations

    Kinesthetic: Physical motion, such as walking around, drawing or building a model.

❏ 3. Help the student set up a dedicated study area, stock it with supplies, and choose tools to encourage focus (gum, stress balls, water bottles, and so forth).

❏ 4. Explain that studying begins when the student first reads the text. Use a social studies or science text to show the student how to read interactively using titles, bolded words, pictures, captions, and bullets to discuss main idea and supporting details.

❏ 5. Discuss effective methods of studying for a quiz or test.

Strategy Three

Strategy Three, Worksheet One

Learning Styles Assessment Questionnaire

A user removable worksheet is available on page 153 of the user worksheet section.

Read each question carefully with your child and then decide together which answer best describes him.

Questions	One	Two	Three
When learning something new in science, do you prefer to:	read the textbook	listen to an explanation	complete an experiment in the science lab
When studying for a spelling test, do you:	try to picture the word in your mind	recite the letters out loud or in your head	write the word to see if it "feels" right
Do you prefer stories with:	good descriptions, so you can picture the scene	good dialogue, so you can understand what is happening between the characters	lots of action, because it is hard to sit still and read
How do you stay focused when listening to a long lecture?	take notes	take no notes but listen closely	take sporadic notes, even if you choose not to use them later
If you are trying to concentrate, do you get distracted by:	clutter or movement nearby	sounds and noises, either too quiet or too loud	activity happening around you
If packing gear for a soccer game (or any extracurricular activity) do you:	make a list in your head or on paper	wait for your mother to call out what you need	just start packing without thinking about it first
When you have a problem, do you:	organize your thoughts with lists	talk to yourself or a friend	engage in a physical activity, like walking around or jogging
When talking to a friend, do you:	like to meet the person face-to-face	prefer to talk on the phone	walk or move around as you talk
If you run into someone you have only met once before, you are most likely to remember:	his face or how he looked	his name or the sound of his voice	his mannerisms or hand motions

INTERPRET YOUR RESULTS!

If most of the responses are ones, your student seems to prefer a visual approach to learning.

If most of the responses are twos, your student seems to prefer an auditory approach to learning.

If most of the responses are threes, your student seems to prefer a kinesthetic approach to learning.

Strategy Three, Worksheet Two

Strategies for the Three Learning Modalities

Strategies for Visual Learners:	Strategies for Auditory Learners:	Strategies for Kinesthetic Learners:
Draw charts, tables, graphs, diagrams, and pictures. • Use Post-it notes. • Use color to highlight important points in a text. • Make lists and categorize information. • Use the computer to make notes or explanations of material. • Practice visualizing information to be memorized.	**Verbalization** • Repeat words aloud. • Read text out loud or have someone read to you. • After reading, summarize key points out loud. • Create musical jingles to aid memorization. • Use verbal analogies and stories to remember key points. • Make speeches and presentations. **Record and Play Back** • Tape record lectures and listen to them as soon as possible after class. • Tape record notes after each class and listen to them later. • Listen to difficult material again and again while traveling, jogging, or doing chores. **Involve Others** • Listen and discuss subject material with others. • Try to teach a younger sibling or explain material to a classmate, parent, or even a pet! • Participate in class discussions as much as possible. • Organize a study group, and discuss material orally. • Ask a lot of questions.	• Keep a stress ball close by to help stay focused. • Touch each finger of your hand to remember five items, both hands for ten items. • Take frequent study breaks to move around. • Use pictures or drawings in combination with writing to take notes in class. • Use movement while studying (e.g., reading while on an exercise bike, molding a piece of clay while learning a new concept, tossing a ball in the air while memorizing, reciting spelling words while riding a bike around the block, jumping rope while repeating math facts). • Try working in different positions, like standing. • Chew gum while studying. • Highlight while reading;

Strategy Three, Worksheet Three

Studying for a Test, Part One

*A user removable worksheet is available
on page 155 of the user worksheet section.*

ON YOUR MARK . . .

Start with Good Studying Habits

1. To really make studying easy, *review your class notes on a weekly basis*. All you have to do is read them over at the end of the week and clarify any confusing information. This ten-minute exercise will help you become familiar with the material and make studying for the test much easier.

2. *Start studying for a test five days in advance and for a quiz, three days.*

3. *Schedule your studying time* on your daily calendar and write down what you will study each night. It is not good enough to write the word "study" in your assignment notebook. Divide your material into manageable parts so that you will have a specific amount of material to cover each night. Plan to finish studying all the material at least two days before the test, so that the night before the test can be devoted to difficult areas and a general review.

4. *Collect all of your information* from class notes, worksheets, textbook, quizzes, and previous tests. If your notes are not complete or legible, copy them from a friend or ask the teacher if you can borrow his notes. When you start far enough ahead of time to prepare for an exam, you have the time to see what is missing or incomplete. Then you have a chance to remedy the situation. Remember, if you only have 70 percent of the information to study, you can only answer 70 percent of the questions!

5. *Create a comprehensive study guide.* Use your class outline or an outline from the textbook as your basis. Then add information from other sources to make a comprehensive outline. As you add information, you are already studying and putting small chunks of information systematically in your brain. This makes retrieval of information much easier. If you are a kinesthetic or auditory learner, talk out loud to anyone who will listen or to yourself as you put all of your information onto one outline. Add additional information in different colors. For example, if you add to your class notes, use green to signify that material is being added from the textbook and use blue to show information added from handouts. This allows you to refer back to the source if there is a question you want to clarify.

You will know about 80 percent of the material when you have finished creating the comprehensive study guide!

Strategy Three, Worksheet Four

Studying for a Test, Part Two

A user removable worksheet is available on page 157 of the user worksheet section.

GET SET . . .

Specific Techniques for Learning the Remaining 20 Percent.

You're on the Home Stretch!

- *Memory strategies* such as visualization, chunking, mnemonics, linking, rhyms, rhythms, and loci will help you remember facts, even under stress. Refer to Strategy Four for specific memory techniques. Rehearse and practice a lot.

- *Flash cards* can be a great studying tool for key terms and vocabulary. If you choose to use note cards, go through the cards daily. The cards that you do not know should be put in a separate pile and reviewed right before you fall asleep and first thing in the morning. These extra few minutes spent reviewing makes memorizing easier.

  Some kids use flash cards for everything. However, if you have a tendency to lose the cards, put the key terms and vocabulary on a sheet of paper. Divide the paper in half using the left side for the term and the right side for the definition.

- *Mind Maps* can help you interact with material to be learned by drawing pictures that represent written information. You can use visual images to help remember the order of events in a historical sequence or for organizing your thoughts on the main idea and details of the material being learned.

- *Timelines* can help you remember dates. Practice writing the dates on a timeline and then go back and fill in the important information about each date. Then explain *why* each date is important.

Strategy Three, Worksheet Five

Studying for a Test, Part Three

A user removable worksheet is available on page 159 of the user worksheet section.

GO!

More Studying Strategies:

- **Form a study group.** In middle school and high school, it is often a good idea to study with others. Although some parents feel that actual work does not take place, study groups offer the opportunity to make sure each student understands the material and has studied in a comprehensive manner. Use the study session to quiz each other on important information and create outlines for possible essay questions. Reward yourself with a pizza or ice cream party *after* the studying is done.

- **Integrate the information.** This may be the hardest task of all. You have to ask yourself why the information is important and how one piece relates to another. Discuss this with other students, especially if you have a hard time understanding the main points and how they relate to the topic you are studying.

- **Prepare for an essay question.** For an essay question, you should prepare to write about *three to five* points about a subject area. Write down how each point you will make relates to the main topic. Provide an example from the material to support each statement.

- **Questions?** Have a sheet ready to jot down questions that you can ask your teacher or a classmate at least two days before the exam. If you keep the sheet with you as you begin studying, your questions will be ready for the teacher. Also, as you become more familiar with the material, you may answer your own questions.

- **The night before** the exam should be for a general review and to go over the more difficult pieces of the material.

- **Any information** that continues to be difficult to memorize should be reviewed once before you go to sleep and then again on the way to the test.

You are ready and well prepared for your test!
Good Luck!

Strategy Three, Worksheet Six

Remember to Do the Following
When Memorizing Material

*A user removable worksheet is available
on page 161 of the user worksheet section.*

1. Start to memorize material as soon as you get it. Remember, memorization takes a lot of repetition.

2. Read the material carefully, to yourself. Are there any pictures you can put in your mind about what you have just read?

3. Repeat the information out loud a lot.

4. Use memorization strategies like visualization, chunking, mnemonics, linking, rhyming, rhythms, and loci. Look for patterns and if you get stuck, try to relate the hard pieces to things that are very familiar to you.

5. Write out the stanza or material you are trying to memorize. Any mistakes should be marked with a very bright color.

6. Repeat and write it again.

7. Now it's time to start cramming. The last two days before the test go over the material as much as possible.

8. The day before the test, review in the afternoon and again before you go to bed.

9. On the day of the test, review first thing in the morning and just before your class.

Strategy Three

Strategy Three, Worksheet Seven

A user removable worksheet is available on page 163 of the user worksheet section.

Use a variety of the studying techniques listed on the worksheets in this Strategy. Reward *each* method used separately to reinforce the value of trying more than one way to interact with material to be learned. Points are also awarded for active reading strategies such as note-taking or highlighting.

Reward Chart

		Monday	Tuesday	Wednesday	Thursday	Friday	Saturday	Sunday
Assignment Notebook	Color coding							
	"Don't Forget" section							
	Writing something in every subject							
	Check/cross check							
Binder	Papers filed							
	Pockets used							
Other	Daily check in/out							
	Time log							
Time Management	Guess/actual time sheets							
	Wearing a watch							
	Using a monthly calendar							
Studying Strategies	Actively Reading							
	New Study Strategy							
	New Study Strategy							

BEFORE MOVING ON . . .

Change is a fact of life, especially in our fast-paced, technological society. Many of the jobs available today did not exist twenty years ago. Knowing how to learn is a skill that your child will utilize his entire life. The ability to acquire new knowledge allows an individual to develop new skills, take up an interesting hobby, or advance his career.

Strategy Four

Memory Strategies

*M*emory is one of the key foundations for learning. Picture a student who listens to a lecture and understands a concept that is explained to her. Without memory, she will never be able to access that concept again or use it in any meaningful way. Without memory, there is no learning. Just like the muscles of your body require constant attention and maintenance to remain strong, memory needs to be exercised regularly to stay in shape. By showing your child how you use your memory for groceries, errands, or a parking space, you are demonstrating that memory is a lifetime skill to be exercised every day.

To help your student learn how to memorize information, teach her a variety of strategies and emphasize that repetition is very important. Practicing different memory techniques and taking time to "over learn" material will teach your child how to store information in her brain in a way that it can be easily retrieved.

GOALS

1. The student will learn different ways to store information in memory.

2. The student will practice various strategies in order to store information for more effective retrieval.

WORKSHEETS

Worksheet One: **Visualization to Improve Memory.** Teach your child novel ways to visualize information to be memorized. This worksheet uses the example of visualizing Florida, which looks like a boot on the map of the United States.

Worksheet Two: **Chunking and Acronyms.** This worksheet will help you demonstrate how to chunk information to be learned and how to create meaningful acronyms.

Worksheet Three: **Combination Approach.** The student will practice using a combination of memory strategies to learn the states along the Mississippi River.

Worksheet Four: **Sample Memory Challenge.** Using the organization of living things, this worksheet demonstrates the use of a variety of memory techniques.

Worksheet Five: **Mind Map for Memorizing the Organization of Living Things.** This sample mind map demonstrates the use of an acrostic and visualization.

Worksheet Six: **Homework and Reward Chart.** Include opportunities to practice memory every day, and reward your child for each new technique practiced. User removable worksheets are available beginning on page 165 of the user worksheet section.

PREPARATION

1. Prepare the worksheets to help you explain each of the memory techniques to your student.

2. Have on-hand supplies to play some memory games. You can use a deck of cards (concentration), several small objects, or a commercial memory game.

Strategy Four

Memory Strategies Checklist

The checklist is a guide to help you progress through each step of teaching memory strategies to your child.

❑ 1. Three kinds of memory—short-term, long-term, and active working memory. Long-term memory is needed for tests and essays, so the student should save time to "over learn" material.

❑ 2. Ways to memorize material:
    Visualization
    Chunking
    Acronyms
    Acrostics
    Rhyme and Rhythm
    Loci
    Combination

❑ 3. Play some memory games with cards, objects, or the alphabet.

Strategy Four, Worksheet One

Visualization to Improve Memory

For practice in visualization: Florida looks like a boot.

Strategy Four, Worksheet Two

Using Chunking and Acronyms

For practice with *chunking* states in a specific region such as the west coast: COW for California, Oregon, and Washington

Strategy Four, Worksheet Three

Combination Approach

For practicing a Combination Approach to Memory:
  Minnesota, Iowa, Missouri, Arkansas, and Louisiana.

- First, use visualization and show the students that the states are in a line running along the Mississippi River.

- Next, look at the first letter in each name to find a pattern, such as C-V-C-V-C (consonant-vowel).

- Create a meaningful acronym for the student, such as "*Mi*nnie *i*s *m*issing *a*nd *l*ate." "Minnie" is used for Minnesota and "missing" for Missouri.

One fifth grader created the following sentence to remember the same states: "My iguana makes awesome lasagna." Because she was fascinated by iguanas and loved to eat lasagna, her crazy sentence stuck in her memory. Five states were learned with one sentence!

Strategy Four, Worksheet Four

Sample Memory Challenge

DIVISIONS OF THE ANIMAL KINGDOM (IN ORDER):

Domain, Kingdom, Phylum, Class, Order, Family, Genus, Species

Acrostic:

Dear King Paul Cried Out For Guts and Slime.

Linking:

In the *Domain* of the *Kingdom*, Sir *Phylum's Class* Made
    Order of Sir *Genus' Species.*

Rhyming:

Domain, Kingdom, Phylum, Class!
    Order, Genus, Species last!

Loci:

Walk around and touch the items to remember the bold words.
       The *Door* is the entrance to my **Domain.**
       The *Bedroom* is my **Kingdom.**
       The *Pillow* is a **Phylum** (both start with P).
       Class is the *Desk* where I do my homework.
       Order is the filing system in my *File Drawer.*
       Genus is the *Paper* in the files (that make me a genius).
       Species is the *Specific Writing* on the papers.

Strategy Four, Worksheet Five

Mind Map

Mind Map for Memorizing the Organization of Living Things Using the Acrostic "Dear King Paul Cried Out for Guts and Slime."

Dear King Paul
(Domain, Kingdom, Phylum)

Cried Out
(Class, Order)

For Guts and Slime
(Family, Genus, Species)

Strategy Four, Worksheet Six

Homework

A user removable worksheet is available on page 165 of the user worksheet section.

Choose a memory challenge and use at least two of the strategies (visualization, chunking, acronyms, acrostics, rhyme and rhythm, loci, and combination) to memorize the information. Here are some ideas for your student's memory challenge:

- U.S. states (One memory challenge could include seven to ten states, such as the Southeast)

- Regional states and capitals

- Five Great Lakes

- List of foreign words

- List of vocabulary words

- Names of all your classmates (name all the girls or all the boys)

- Names of all the neighbors on your street

- Your family genealogy: list the names of your family members, aunts, uncles, cousins, and grandparents

- A section of the Periodic Table of Elements

- Grocery list (make up your own)

Reward Chart

Strategy Four, Worksheet Six

A user removable worksheet is available on page 167 of the user worksheet section.

		Monday	Tuesday	Wednesday	Thursday	Friday	Saturday	Sunday
Assignment Notebook	Color coding							
	"Don't Forget" section							
	Writing something in every subject							
	Check/cross check							
Binder	Papers filed							
	Pockets used							
Other	Daily check in/out							
Time Management	Time log							
	Guess/actual time sheets							
	Wearing a watch							
	Using a monthly calendar							
Studying Strategies	Actively reading							
	New Study Strategy							
	New Study Strategy							
Memory	Memory Strategy							
	Memory Strategy							
	Memory Strategy							

Strategy Four

BEFORE MOVING ON . . .

Some people just seem to be born with good memories. However, most of us need to practice this skill over time in order to improve the ability to retain information in memory and retrieve it at will. The more your student practices, the stronger her memory will become. Encourage her by practicing with games, and you will both be exercising your "memory muscles."

Strategy Five

Note-Taking to Improve Reading Comprehension

Taking notes helps the student better understand written material. As he creates notes, he is deciding what is important and is also condensing material into manageable sections. The student stays engaged with his reading material and focused on determining the main ideas and supporting facts. The act of note-taking can improve the student's reading comprehension and facilitate the integration of material to be learned.

There are many note-taking systems available, however, while learning to take notes in the *Thinking Organized*™ program, the student should only use the note-taking systems provided here. A student who presents with organizational challenges needs clear direction without options. Once the skills become habit, the student can substitute another outlining system, thereby individualizing the program.

GOALS

Learn to determine the main idea and supporting details from a written passage by taking notes.

1. Two-Column Outlining System

2. Cornell Outlining System

WORKSHEETS

Worksheet One: **Blank Two-Column Note-taking Sheet.** List a key word or phrase on the left side of the page (the main idea) and use the right side of the page for the supporting information. Use one color for the main ideas and another color for the supporting information. User removable worksheets are available on page 169 of the user worksheet section.

Worksheet Two: **Image One to Practice Two-Column Note-Taking.** This simple image will help you practice finding a main idea and supporting information with your student. A user removable worksheet is available on page 173 of the user worksheet section.

Worksheet Three: **Sample Two-Column Notes for Image One.** This is a sample of an appropriate main idea and supporting information for Image One.

Worksheet Four: **Image Two to Practice Two-Column Note-Taking.** This worksheet will help you practice finding a main idea and supporting information with your student, using a more detailed image. A user removable worksheet is available on page 174 of the user worksheet section.

Worksheet Five: **Sample Notes for Image Two.** This is a sample of an appropriate main idea and supporting information for Image Two.

Worksheet Six: **Image Three to Practice Two-Column Note-Taking.** This simple image will help you practice finding a main idea and supporting information with your student. A user removable worksheet is available on page 175 of the user worksheet section.

Worksheet Seven: **Sample Two-Column Notes for Image Three.** This is a sample of an appropriate main idea and supporting information for Image Three.

Worksheet Eight: **Image Four to Practice Two-Column Note-Taking.** This simple image will help you practice finding a main idea and supporting information with your student. A user removable worksheet is available on page 176 of the user worksheet section.

Worksheet Nine: **Sample Two-Column Notes for Image Four.** This is a sample of an appropriate main idea and supporting information for Image Four.

Worksheet Ten: **Image Five to Practice Two-Column Note-Taking.** This simple image will help you practice finding a main idea and supporting information with your student. User removable worksheets are available on page 177 of the user worksheet section.

Worksheet Eleven: **Sample Two-Column Notes for Image Five.** This is a sample of an appropriate main idea and supporting information for Image Five.

Worksheet Twelve: **Image Six to Practice Two-Column Note-Taking.** This simple image will help you practice finding a main idea and supporting information with your student. A user removable worksheet is available on page 178 of the user worksheet section.

Worksheet Thirteen: **Sample Two-Column Notes for Image Six.** This is a sample of an appropriate main idea and supporting information for Image Six.

Worksheet Fourteen: **Image Seven to Practice Two-Column Note-Taking.** This simple image will help you practice finding a main idea and supporting information with your student. A user removable worksheet is available on page 179 of the user worksheet section.

Worksheet Fifteen: **Sample Two-Column Notes for Image Seven.** This is a sample of an appropriate main idea and supporting information for Image Seven.

Worksheet Sixteen: **Cornell Outlining System.** Copies of this worksheet are provided for you to use with your student. List a main idea on the left side of the paper with a key word or phrase. On the right-hand side of the paper, give a statement that supports the main idea. List details underneath the supporting ideas. The two-inch margin at the bottom of the paper is for a one- to two-sentence summary of the information that was outlined above. User removable worksheets are available beginning on page 181 of the user worksheet section.

Worksheet Seventeen: **Sample Paragraph to Practice Note-taking Skills.** This worksheet will help you practice note-taking with a well-organized paragraph of text.

Worksheet Eighteen: **Sample Notes from Paragraph.** This is a sample of an appropriate Two-Column Note-taking system for the sample paragraph in Worksheet Seventeen.

Worksheet Nineteen: **Sample Cornell Outline.** This is a sample of an appropriate Cornell Outline for the sample paragraph in Worksheet Seventeen.

Worksheet Twenty: **Sample Essay to Practice Cornell Outlining System.** This worksheet will help you practice the Cornell Outlining System with a well-organized essay.

Worksheet Twenty-One: **Sample Cornell Outline from Essay.** This is a sample of an appropriate Cornell Outline for the sample paragraph in Worksheet Nineteen.

Worksheet Twenty-Two: **Homework and Reward Chart.** Practice note-taking with an actual reading assignment or a passage in a social studies textbook, and reward the student's efforts. User removable worksheets are available beginning on page 185 of the user worksheet section.

PREPARATION

It will be helpful to have these supplies handy to practice note-taking techniques with your child.

1. Several sheets of lined paper or a blank document on the computer

2. Pencils or pens

3. Social studies or science textbook or any non-fiction text that is not too difficult for your child to read and understand

Strategy Five

Note-Taking for Reading Comprehension Checklist

The checklist is a guide to help you progress through each step of teaching note-taking for reading comprehension to your child.

❏ 1. Practice getting the main idea and supporting details from an image by taking notes with the Two-Column note-taking system:

    Main idea on left

    Supporting details on right

❏ 2. Practice getting the main idea and supporting details from a written passage by taking notes with the Cornell Outlining System

    Main idea or key words on left

    Supporting details on right (pictures are good too!)

    One or two sentence summary at bottom for quick review later

Strategy Five, Worksheet One

User removable worksheets are available beginning on page 169 of the user worksheet section.

Blank Two-Column Note-taking Sheet

Main Idea	Details

©2008, Rhona M. Gordon, Thinking Organized™. All Rights Reserved. Duplication permitted by owner of *Thinking Organized for Parents and Children Workbook*

Strategy Five

Strategy Five

Strategy Five, Worksheet Two

Image One to Practice Two-Column Note-taking System

A user removable worksheet is available on page 173 of the user worksheet section.

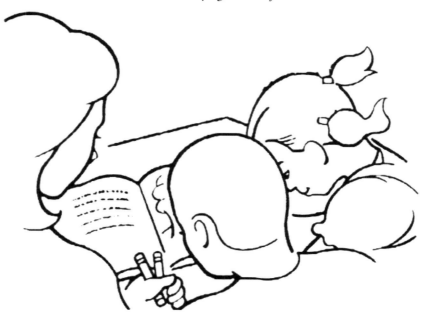

Main Idea	Details

Strategy Five, Worksheet Three

Image One to Practice Two-Column Note-taking System

Main Idea	Details
A boy and a girl are reading and coloring a book while the mother watches.	Boy—holding two crayons
	Girl—concentrating on book
	Mother—standing behind children

Strategy Five, Worksheet Four

Image Two to Practice Two-Column Note-Taking

A user removable worksheet is available on page 174 of the user worksheet section.

Main Idea	Details

Strategy Five, Worksheet Five

Sample Notes for Image Two

Main Idea	Details
The boy is getting dressed to go outside to play in the snow.	Boy—putting on jacket Mom—putting on boy's hat
	Scarf and mittens on chair Sled in front of boy
	*Background: Snow falling Snow on tree and ground

Note: Although at first it is best to limit your student to three details, as he grows more proficient at finding the main ideas and supporting details, it is helpful to have him add more information. Details relating to the background of an image are a good place to start, because these help him examine the image more closely.

Strategy Five, Worksheet Six

Image Three to Practice Two-Column Note-Taking

A user removable worksheet is available on page 175 of the user worksheet section.

Main Idea	Details

Strategy Five, Worksheet Seven

Sample Notes for Image Three

Main Idea	Details
A girl is playing in the sandbox.	Girl—wearing short dress with large dots 　　—hair is short and black 　　—scooping sand into pail 　　—left foot buried in sand
	Background—ladder is leaning (don't know what it's leaning against). Four rungs of ladder are visible
	Foreground—clumps of grass on the left and right side of the sandbox.

Strategy Five, Worksheet Eight

Image Four to Practice Two-Column Note-Taking

A user removable worksheet is available on page 176 of the user worksheet section.

Main Idea	Details

Strategy Five, Worksheet Nine

Sample Notes for Image Four

Main Idea	Details
The children have almost finished building a snowman.	Girl—patting snowman's neck 　　—facing the snowman and her face can't be seen
	Boy—patting snowman's chest 　　—behind the snowman, face can be seen Snowman—has buttons, eyes, nose, and mouth 　　—missing his left ear
	Foreground—three snowballs in front of the snowman and one near the boy Background—barren tree branch on left side

Strategy Five, Worksheet Ten

Image Five to Practice Two-Column Note-Taking

A user removable worksheet is available on page 177 of the user worksheet section.

Main Idea	Details

Strategy Five, Worksheet Eleven

Sample Notes for Image Five

Main Idea	Details
Six high school students are working at their desks in a classroom while the teacher watches from behind.	Three boys in right-hand row holding pencils, concentrating on their papers
	Boy in the back, middle of the classroom reading his paper
	Girl on left side of classroom holding her pencil and sitting with her elbows on the desk

Strategy Five, Worksheet Twelve

Image Six to Practice Two-Column Note-Taking

A user removable worksheet is available on page 178 of the user worksheet section.

Main Idea	Details

Strategy Five, Worksheet Thirteen

Sample Notes for Image Six

Main Idea	Details
A man is playing a guitar while a girl dances and a boy claps.	Man—sitting on chair with right leg crossed over left
	Boy—kneeling on ground to the left of the man and clapping

	Girl—dancing to the right of the man and swirling her dress
	
	    —feet are bare
	    —braids flying out behind her

Note: To go even further, you could add details as to the man's moustache, his suit and tie, his black shoes, his chair, the boy's clothing, the ruffles on the girl's dress, and the background plants.

Strategy Five, Worksheet Fourteen

Image Seven to Practice Two-Column Note-Taking

A user removable worksheet is available on page 179 of the user worksheet section.

Main Idea	Details

Strategy Five, Worksheet Fifteen

Sample Notes for Image Seven

Main Idea	Details
The boy is sick in bed and the mother is comforting him.	Boy—thermometer in mouth Teddy bear—lying to the left of the boy under covers —big bow on side of neck
	Car, crayons, and a book resting on top of the covers
	Mom is kneeling on right side of bed with right hand on boy's head, her left hand on the covers

Cornell Outlining System

Strategy Five, Worksheet Sixteen

User removable worksheets are available beginning on page 181 of the user worksheet section.

Key Phrase or Word	Main Idea	Supporting Idea
		Supporting Idea
		Detail
		Detail
		Supporting Idea
		Detail
		Detail
		Short Summary:

Strategy Five, Worksheet Seventeen

Sample Paragraph to Practice Note-Taking Skills

There is a new kind of corn developed by cross breeding that could be effective in helping farmers grow better corn. In the past, farmers have had a difficult time raising corn, and therefore appreciate scientists' efforts to help them grow sturdier plants with better yields. The new plants grow quickly, thereby increasing productivity. Because they are larger and faster growing, they are more resistant to bugs and other diseases. Each plant produces 30 percent more corn. Therefore, farmers get more corn per plant, more growing time, and fewer problems.

Main Idea	Details

Strategy Five, Worksheet Eighteen

Sample Notes from Paragraph

There is a new kind of corn developed by cross breeding that could be effective in helping farmers grow better corn. In the past, farmers have had a difficult time raising corn, and therefore appreciate scientists' efforts to help them grow sturdier plants with better yields. The new plants grow quickly, thereby increasing productivity. Because they are larger and faster growing, they are more resistant to bugs and other diseases. Each plant produces 30 percent more corn. Therefore, farmers get more corn per plant, more growing time, and fewer problems.

Main Idea	Details
Better corn developed by cross breeding	Grows quickly, thereby increasing productivity
	More resistant to bugs and disease
	Produces 30 percent more

Strategy Five, Worksheet Nineteen

Cornell Outlining System

Key Phrase or Word
Improving Corn

Main Idea
Better corn developed by cross breeding

Supporting Idea
Farmers need sturdier plants

Detail
Grows quickly, thereby increasing productivity

Detail
More resistant to bugs and disease

Detail
Produces 30 percent more

Short Summary:
Cross breeding has been successfully used to produce corn that is stronger and more plentiful than the older plants.

Strategy Five

Strategy Five, Worksheet Twenty

Sample Essay to Practice Cornell Outlining System

Parents and teachers complain that video games are a waste of time. Often children must earn the right to play video games. However, video games can be considered good for children, and it is time to think about the positive aspects of this pastime. Playing video games can build academic and social skills while the player is having fun.

Modern video games incorporate many educational skills. Some games use real-life situations that can improve logic and decision-making skills. There are several simulation games in which the player designs and runs a company, war, theme park, or household. To do this, the gamer must continually consider future consequences and think ahead of the actual play. In order to be successful at these games, the player needs to make fast decisions based on logical consequences that have been learned not only from the game but also in real life.

Another educational skill practiced in video games is memory. Most games require the player to hold information in memory while working toward the ultimate goal. Today's video games can have as many as 150 characters that need to be remembered and used by the player. Even if the game takes several sessions to complete, the player has to recall who is good and who is evil, as well as each character's individual strengths and weaknesses. Many times the player must keep in mind a large map in order to move his character to different places. When the gamer is required to remember information both during a game and from session to session, he is using repetition, mind maps, and visualization to memorize and recall the information necessary to beat the game.

Video games also build children's social skills. Children who play video games become less shy in social situations. Most adults do not understand the language of video games, but knowing about a popular game gives even a shy kid confidence to talk to friends. Sometimes a gamer will become more accepted because he figured out a secret to a popular game. When children discover they share an interest in video games, they have a common foundation to form a friendship.

It is time to recognize that video games can help teach skills needed to do well in school, and can help children socially. Therefore, parents and teachers should not limit video game playing too severely, or worry when their children play a lot of video games. Maybe they will actually learn something!

Strategy Five, Worksheet Twenty-One

Sample Cornell Outline from Essay on Worksheet Twenty

Key Phrase or Word	Main Idea
Video games are worthwhile	Playing video games can build academic, memory, and social skills, while the player is having fun.

Supporting Idea
Educational: improve logic and decision-making skills

    Detail
    Simulation games: run a company, war, theme park, or household

    Detail
    Consider consequences, think ahead

    Detail
    Make fast decisions based on game and real life

Supporting Idea
Memory skills practiced

    Detail
    Must remember overall map to move characters around

    Detail
    Uses repetition, mind maps, and visualization

Supporting Idea
Builds social skills

    Detail
    Makes kids less shy—unique language for games

    Detail
    Gives confidence when figuring out a secret to a game

    Detail
    Gives common foundation for friendship

Short Summary:
Although many parents think video games are a waste of time, they can improve logic and decision-making skills, expand memory techniques, and help children grow socially.

Strategy Five

Strategy Five

Homework

Strategy Five, Worksheet Twenty-Two

User removable worksheets are available beginning on page 185 of the user worksheet section.

Have the student practice the Two-Column note-taking system or the Cornell Outlining System on an assignment from school or a social studies or science textbook chapter. See how much the student can do independently, but do not hesitate to help. Remember that it takes a great deal of practice and repetition before a student can take effective notes.

Reward Chart

		Monday	Tuesday	Wednesday	Thursday	Friday	Saturday	Sunday
Assignment Notebook	Color coding							
	"Don't Forget" section							
	Writing something in every subject							
	Check/cross check							
Binder	Papers filed							
	Pockets used							
Other	Daily check in/out							
	Time log							
Time Management	Guess/actual time sheets							
	Wearing a watch							
	Using a monthly calendar							
Studying Strategies	Actively Reading							
	New Study Strategy							
	New Study Strategy							
Memory	Memory Strategy							
	Memory Strategy							
	Memory Strategy							
Note-Taking	Practice taking notes							

BEFORE MOVING ON . . .

Note-taking, like most of the skills in the *Thinking Organized*™ program, needs lots of practice to help the student become proficient. Main ideas and details can be discussed verbally from other sources than just textbooks. Movies and TV shows provide a chance to practice this skill. Parents should point out to their children that subject matter can be looked at from the details leading to the main idea or the main idea leading to the supporting details. This helps children see material from more than one perspective, which in turn encourages flexible thinking.

Strategy Six

Written Language Skills

*L*earning to write in clear and precise language is a challenge at any developmental level, and as a student progresses through the elementary grades into middle school and high school, the writing assignments increase in number and complexity. Having a specific pattern to follow gives the student a way to begin writing and helps her to produce a more organized essay.

A student who is disorganized is often amazed that ideas form so easily in her head but become very difficult to put on paper. Therefore, this strategy begins with ways to get started writing. Brainstorming for ideas, with either the child or a parent taking notes, can be an effective way to begin the flow of ideas. Other methods include having the child develop questions to be answered, or using a CLOZE activity. The CLOZE procedure helps the student outline parts of an essay by creating key sentences with a significant piece left blank. Parental help will be needed in developing the sentences initially. Older students can be taught to create a mind map. In the middle of the mind map is the central concept of the essay, which becomes the basis of the introduction. Stemming from the central concept are the supporting arguments or facts, each of which may become the topic sentence of a paragraph. The remainder of the web provides evidence and examples to explain each argument.

Having a formal structure to follow gives the student a way to begin writing and helps her to produce a more organized essay. To introduce writing formats, explain the umbrella structure of organized writing to your student. In writing an effective paragraph, the top of the umbrella becomes the introductory sentence, the supports are examples and explanations, decorations are descriptive details, and the handle is the closing sentence. Once the student learns to write an effective paragraph, have her apply the umbrella structure to her entire essay.

As the student's writing increases in length and complexity, the S.E.E. approach becomes a more effective structure. In each of the body paragraphs, the student should write a topic sentence that will be the overview of that paragraph. Next the student should follow the S.E.E. structure:

- **S:** Statement. Make a statement about the topic sentence that you will prove.

- **E:** Evidence. Give evidence or examples from general knowledge, text material, or research.

- **E:** Explanation. Tell the reader why the evidence chosen supports the initial statement. This step is often omitted, but it is extremely important!

For more detailed explanations and ideas on how to customize writing strategies to the age of your child, it is important to refer to Strategy Six in *Thinking Organized for Parents and Children.*

GOALS

1. *Pre-writing strategies* will help the student get started planning her essay in an organized format.

2. *A writing structure* provides an easy-to-follow framework for the student's ideas.

3. *Preparing for essay questions* will help the student produce organized essays that incorporate critical thinking and analysis.

4. *Writing a research paper* requires a student to integrate planning, researching, note-taking, organizing, writing, and editing skills.

WORKSHEETS

Worksheet One: **Questions to Help You Get Started Writing Using the Sample Prompt, "Video Games Are Worthwhile" Blank Form.** A user removable worksheet is available on page 187 of the user worksheet section.

Worksheet Two: **Questions to Help You Get Started Writing Using the Sample Prompt, "Video Games Are Worthwhile."** This worksheet demonstrates how a student can use questions to generate ideas for writing, using the example of "Video Games are Worthwhile."

Worksheet Three: **Practice CLOZE Activity.** Using the same example of "Video Games Are Worthwhile," this worksheet shows the use of the CLOZE procedure by developing key sentences with the endings left blank. If the student can complete a CLOZE sheet, she has effectively visualized and outlined the entire essay. A user removable worksheet is available on page 188 of the user worksheet section.

Worksheet Four: **Sample Mind Map For "Video Games are Worthwhile."** This worksheet shows a student how a mind map can help her generate ideas and specific evidence to back up those ideas, forming the basis for an organized essay.

Worksheet Five: **Sample Mind Map for an Essay about** *One Flew over the Cuckoo's Nest*. This mind map demonstrates an outline for a more sophisticated and elaborate essay about rebellion and conformity in *One Flew over the Cuckoo's Nest*.

Worksheet Six: **Umbrella Structure of Organized Writing.** This worksheet will help you demonstrate how a well-organized paragraph needs a topic sentence, main idea, evidence, explanation, details, and a concluding sentence.

Worksheet Seven: **Sample Use of Umbrella Structure of Organized Writing.** The umbrella structure is illustrated with a sample paragraph from an essay on video games.

Worksheet Eight: **S.E.E. Your Way to Success!** Use this worksheet to help your student understand the S.E.E. (Statement, Evidence, Explanation) structure of organized writing.

Worksheet Nine: **S.E.E. Example for Elementary and Middle School Students.** This essay will help you point out how the S.E.E. structure of organized writing was effectively used in an essay proving the worth of video games.

Worksheet Ten: **S.E.E. Example for High School Students.** An excerpt from an actual eleventh-grade essay, this worksheet demonstrates the use of the S.E.E. structure with higher-level writing.

Worksheet Eleven: **Preparing for an Essay Test.** A quick guide to help you organize your thoughts for any one of the four kinds of essays.

Worksheet Twelve: **Writing a Research Paper, Step-by-Step.** From scheduling to the final check, this quick review leads you through the steps of writing a great research paper.

Worksheet Thirteen: **Dos and Don'ts of Great Writing.** This is a quick guide to improving your student's writing. It is helpful to post this worksheet where the student is actually doing the writing.

Worksheet Fourteen: **Writing for Elementary School Students.** If your student is in elementary school, keep this worksheet of handy tips where she will be writing.

Worksheet Fifteen: **Writing for Middle School Students.** If your student is in middle school, keep this worksheet of handy tips where she will be writing.

Worksheet Sixteen: **Writing for High School Students.** If your student is in high school, keep this worksheet of handy tips where she will be writing.

Worksheet Seventeen: **Final Check.** Encourage your student to use this worksheet after she is finished writing, to edit the document one last time before asking a parent, teacher, or trusted friend to proofread.

Worksheet Eighteen: **Homework and Reward Chart.** Reward your student each time she practices one of the writing strategies you have introduced and practiced together. User removable worksheets are available beginning on page 189 of the user worksheet section.

PREPARATION

It will be helpful to have these supplies handy to help your child practice effective written language:

1. Several sheets of lined paper or a document on the computer

2. Pencils or pens

3. Index cards and a large envelope, if writing a research paper

Strategy Six

Written Language Skills Checklist

The checklist is a guide to help you progress through each step of teaching written language skills to your child. Some of these items are accompanied by a specific worksheet, while other strategies are detailed in *Thinking Organized for Parents and Children, Helping Kids Get Organized for Home, School and Play.*

❏ 1. Introduce techniques to help a writer get started:

   Creative Writing

   • Use visualization to picture ideas for writing.

   • Writing about things that are familiar.

   Expository Writing

   • Brainstorming, writing out ideas

   • Asking questions to get started

   • CLOZE activities

   • Mind map

❏ 2. Writing an Introduction

   • Picture a funnel that goes from broad to narrow.

   • Younger students will develop a topic sentence for the main idea of a paragraph.

   • Older students will develop a thesis.

❏ 3. Introduce Writing Structure

   • Umbrella

   • S.E.E. (Statement, Evidence, Explanation)

❏ 4. Conclusion

- Restate main ideas of paper

- Give a "So What?"

❏ 5. Final Check

- Grammar, punctuation, and spelling

- Transition sentences between paragraphs

- Use a buddy

❏ 6. Preparing for an Essay Test

- Brainstorm possible topics

- Determine main idea and supporting details

- Write sample organizers

❏ 7. The Research Paper

- Set a schedule

- Choose a topic

- Research

- Take notes

- Develop a thesis

- Outline

- Write

- Edit and revise

Strategy Six, Worksheet One

Questions to Help You Get Started Writing Using the Sample Prompt, "Video Games are Worthwhile"

A user removable worksheet is available on page 187 of the user worksheet section.

What do you like about video games?

_____

_____

_____

What do you know about video games?

_____

_____

_____

Do video games involve any useful skills?

_____

_____

_____

Why are video games worthwhile?

_____

_____

_____

_____

Strategy Six, Worksheet Two

Questions to Help You Get Started Writing Using the Sample Prompt, "Video Games are Worthwhile"

What do you like about video games?

Games with stories, where you have to go through different levels

Being inside, playing with my friends

Talking about video games with my friends

What do you know about video games?

Mom always knows where I am

I have strong fingers now and can do other finger things faster

My friend's brother got a job drawing for a video game company

Do video games involve any useful skills?

Good memory, fast fingers, eye-hand coordination

Reading instructions, keep trying until you figure out a level

Why are video games worthwhile?

Educational—have to think to play and learn about story lines and characters

Social development—play and interact with friends

Good for eye-hand coordination and finger muscles

Possible future job or job skill

Strategy Six, Worksheet Three

Practice CLOZE Activity

A user removable worksheet is available on page 188 of the user worksheet section.

Three things I like about video games are _____,

_____, and _____. Two things that

video games teach are _____ and

_____. My mother likes video games because

_____ and _____. I also

think video games are a good thing because _____ and _____

_____.

Strategy Six, Worksheet Four

Sample Mind Map for "Video Games Are Worthwhile"

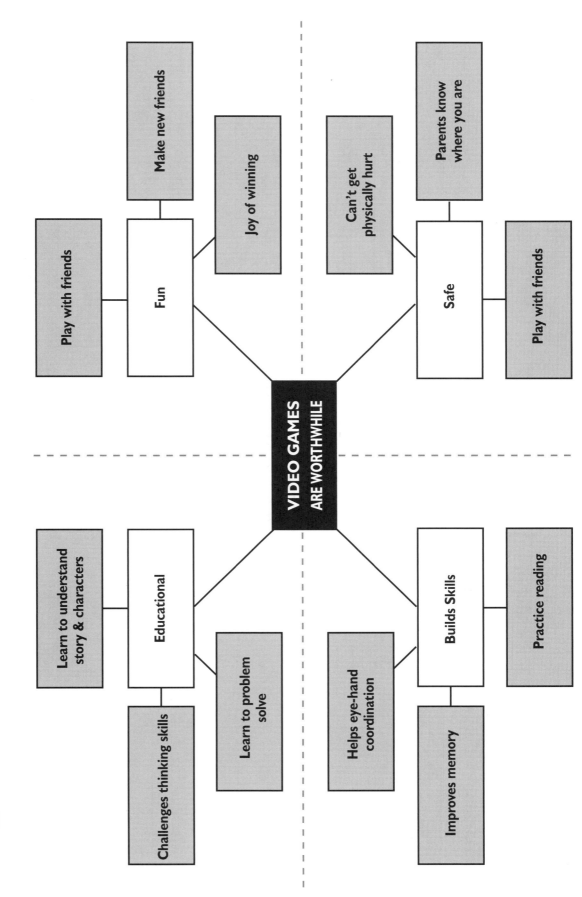

Strategy Six, Worksheet Five

Sample Mind Map for an Essay about *One Flew over the Cuckoo's Nest*

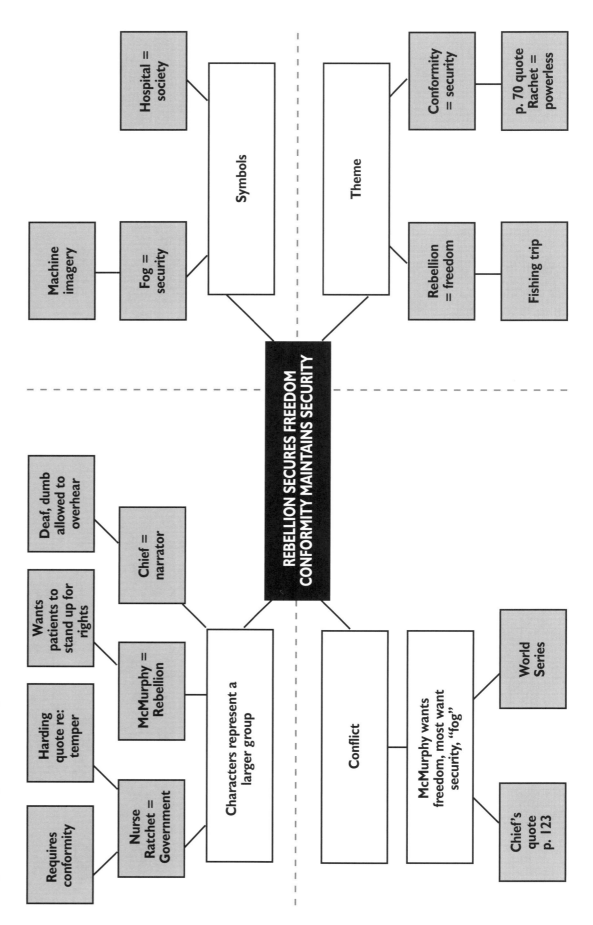

Strategy Six, Worksheet Six

The Umbrella Structure of Organized Writing

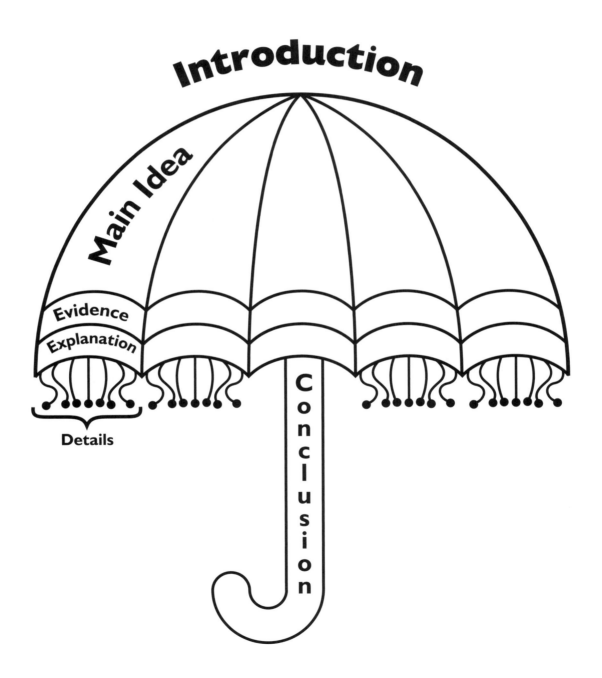

Strategy Six, Worksheet Seven

Sample Use of Umbrella Structure of Organized Writing

Paragraph: Another educational skill practiced in video games is memory. Most games require the player to hold information in memory while working toward the ultimate goal. Today's video games can have as many as 150 characters that need to be remembered and used by the player. Even if the game takes several sessions to complete, the player has to recall who is good and who is evil. The hardest to remember are the evil characters, because they all look alike. When the gamer is required to remember these characters, he is using repetition, mind maps, and visualization to memorize and recall information necessary to beat the game.

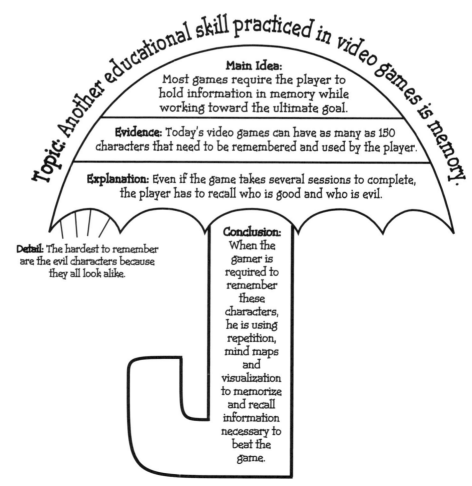

Strategy Six, Worksheet Eight

S.E.E. Your Way to Success!

EXPOSITORY WRITING

Writing for the purpose of *explaining*
You must *prove* something
You will prove your *thesis statement*
You must use *evidence* or specific examples

This is the type of writing you will need to do on essay tests and in English and history classes, so let's try to make this easy.

Follow this advice:

Introduction: Be sure the thesis is the last sentence of your introductory paragraph.

Paragraph: Topic sentence must be an overview of the paragraph and must relate to your thesis.

S: Statement: Make a statement about the topic sentence that you will prove.

E: Evidence: Give examples or quotes to support your statement.

E: Explanation: Explain how your evidence proves your point. This proof should relate directly to your thesis.

Strategy Six, Worksheet Nine

S.E.E. Example for Elementary and Middle School Students

Strategy Six

VIDEO GAMES ARE WORTHWHILE

Start with general look at topic	Parents and teachers complain that video games are a waste of time. Often children must earn the right to play video games. However, video games can be considered good for children, and it is time to think about the positive aspects of this pastime. Playing video games can build academic and social skills, while the player is having fun.
Present Problem	
Introduce Main Idea or Thesis	
TOPIC	Modern video games incorporate many educational skills. Some games use real-life situations that can improve logic and decision-making skills. There are several simulation games in which the player designs and runs a company, war, theme park, or household. To do this, the gamer must continually consider future consequences and think ahead of the actual play.* In order to be successful at these games, the player needs to make fast decisions based on logical consequences that have been learned not only from the game but also in real life.
STATEMENT	
EVIDENCE	
EXPLANATION	
TOPIC	Another educational skill practiced in video games is memory. Most games require the player to hold information in memory while working toward the ultimate goal. Today's video games can have as many as 150 characters that need to be remembered and used by the player. Even if the game takes several sessions to complete, the player has to recall who is good and who is evil, as well as each character's individual strengths and weaknesses. Many times the player must keep in mind the large map in order to move his character to different places. When the gamer is required to remember information both during a game and from session to session, he is using repetition, mind maps and visualization to memorize and recall the information necessary to beat the game.
STATEMENT	
EVIDENCE	
EXPLANATION	
TOPIC	Video games also build children's social skills. Children who play video games become less shy in social situations. Most adults do not understand the language of video games, but knowing about a popular game gives even a shy kid confidence to talk to friends. Sometimes a gamer will be become more accepted because he figured out a secret to a popular game. When children discover they share an interest in video games, they have a common foundation to form a friendship.
STATEMENT	
EVIDENCE	
EXPLANATION	
Conclusion: Restate Thesis	It is time to recognize that video games can help teach skills needed to do well in school, and can help children socially. Therefore, parents and teachers should not limit video game playing too severely, or worry when their children play a lot of video games. Maybe they will actually learn something!
Then add meaning - the "so what?"	

In a student's actual essay, it would be necessary to mention specific games by name in order to provide proper evidence.

Strategy Six, Worksheet Ten

S.E.E. Example for High School Students

The following is an excerpt from an actual eleventh-grade essay. Included in this writing is the introductory paragraph along with two subsequent paragraphs that show the student's ability to use the S.E.E. structure in his writing. The essay has not been edited to perfection, but is presented as an actual example of a student who previously struggled with the writing process and learned to create an organized essay by using the S.E.E. structure.

REBELLION VS. CONFORMITY IN
ONE FLEW OVER THE CUCKOO'S NEST

Start with general look at topic	Freedom is a concept that comes when one stands up for oneself and is not held down by the constraints of others. However, this freedom comes at a high price and no guarantees for success. One might be dissatisfied with the governing body or those who have direct influence over one's life. Rebellion can occur to gain freedom from unhappiness, or one can conform to those in control to maintain the secure environment. Ken Kesey in *One Flew Over the Cuckoo's Nest* conveys the need for rebellion to secure freedom versus conformity to maintain security through the use of characters, conflict and symbols.
Present Problem	
Introduce Main Idea or Thesis	
TOPIC STATEMENT	One character in this novel can play the role of another person or a large group of people within society. The "Big Nurse" or Nurse Rachet in the story portrays the evil, suppressive government. She sets the rules and regulations that are similar to society's judicial structure. She shows the controlling side of the government and how the government keeps one in line in order to maintain control over the population. The nurse requires conformity from her patients. When one of the patients named Harding says, "You're safe as long as you keep control. As long as you don't lose your temper and give her actual reason to request the restriction of the Disturbed Ward, or the therapeutic benefits of Electro Shock, you are safe. But that entails first and foremost keeping one's temper." (Kesey 71) This shows that the nurse, like the government, will punish you if you do not abide by the set standards. Just like the patients must conform to Nurse Rachet's rules, citizens in a society must follow the law of the government.
EVIDENCE	
EXPLANATION	

continued on next page

continued from previous page

TRANSITION SENTENCE

TOPIC

STATEMENT

EVIDENCE

EXPLANATION

The characters in the story help to illustrate some of the conflicts in society.

Kesey shows how conflicts in the ward mirror those of society. Freedom vs. Security is a large conflict in the novel. McMurphy wants freedom along with some of the other patients, but most of the patients prefer the security of the hospital ward. The security is sometimes called the "fog." When the chief tells the reader that, "As bad as it is, you can slip back in it and feel safe. That's what McMurphy can't understand, us wanting to be safe. He keeps trying to drag us out of the fog, out in the open where we'd be easy to get at." (Kesey 123) The patients want the security that "the fog" provides in favor of the high painful cost of freedom. When the chief tells the reader about McMurphy's desire to watch the World Series the nurse says no. "This doesn't surprise him, coming from the nurse; what does surprise him is how the Acutes act when he asks them what they think of the idea. "Nobody says a thing. They're all sunk back out of sight in little pockets of fog. I can barely see them." (Kesey 114) McMurphy is frustrated by the reaction of the patients and their unwillingness to stand up for themselves against Nurse Rachet. In McMurphy's mind the rules are arbitrary and only in place for the sake of controlling the patients. He feels that the Acutes should reject these illogical rules, yet he is disappointed when they stay in the fog. The conflicts lead to a clear struggle between rebellion and conformity.

Strategy Six, Worksheet Eleven

Preparing for an Essay Test

WHAT TO DO:

- Determine several main ideas and supporting details from your notes and textbook.

- Brainstorm for sample essay questions from each of the *Kinds of Essay Questions* below.

- Draw written connections between key points for each sample question. You can use pictures and different colors, just don't get carried away with the artwork!

- Prepare sample outlines using the S.E.E. structure of organized writing.

- *You are ready for your essay test!*

KINDS OF ESSAY QUESTIONS:

1. **Factual Questions:** Describe, define, outline, or explain. For example: *Describe the events leading up to WWII.*

2. **Analyze and Interpret Questions:** Use facts but also link information using some inferential thinking. For example: *Analyze the events leading up to WWII.*

3. **Opinion Questions:** Make your own opinion about the facts and provide details to support your point of view. For example: *Why do you think this happened?* or *What changes in events leading up to WWII do you think would have prevented an increase in hostility?*

4. **Compare and Contrast Questions:** Brainstorm for key similarities and differences. For example: *Compare and contrast the events leading up to WWII from the perspective of the Axis and Allies.*

Strategy Six, Worksheet Twelve

Writing a Research Paper, Step-by-Step

1. **Set a Schedule:** Plan *backwards* by first writing the due date on the calendar, then including a date for the completion of the final edit, proofreading, rough draft, research, and topic choice.

2. **Choose a Topic:** Ask yourself a lot of questions to narrow down a specific topic to be addressed. Then check to be sure it meets the criteria of the assignment.

3. **Research:** Be sure to print all Internet research so you will be able to reference.

4. **Take Notes on Index Cards or in a Notebook:**
   a. List one fact per card or page
   b. List the source on the card or page.
   c. Separate notes by topic.
   d. Double-check after each research session.
   e. Keep your notes safe in an envelope that closes securely!

5. **Develop a Thesis Statement:** Tell the reader what you are trying to prove.

6. **Outline:** Use a web, bullet points, or informal outline to organize ideas.

7. **Write:**
   a. First write body paragraphs, using the S.E.E. method.
   b. Leave the introduction and conclusion for last.

8. **Proofread and Edit:** Use *Worksheet Sixteen, Final Check* for your last thorough proofreading, and then use the buddy system for a parent or teacher to read the paper for a final edit.

Strategy Six, Worksheet Thirteen

Dos and Don'ts of Great Writing

DO:

1. Remember it is the writer's job to make the reader understand the writer's train of thought. The reader should not have to guess at what the writer is trying to express.

2. Break up long paragraphs into two (or more) smaller ones. Make your paragraph breaks in logical places. A paragraph should not fill an entire piece of paper when you are typing your essay.

3. Use transition sentences between the paragraphs so that each paragraph is connected to the next instead of making the reader connect the thoughts.

4. Analyze a point rather than retell the story.

DO NOT:

1. Use "I," "We," or "You" in a formal, expository essay.

2. Introduce a quote with, "On page 35, So-and-so says . . ."

3. Begin an essay with sentences like, "In this essay I will show that . . ." or "The purpose of this essay is to prove that . . ."

4. End a paragraph with a quote.

5. Use quotes without explaining them.

6. Never use the words "thing" or "stuff." They are too vague and do not convey an idea.

Strategy Six, Worksheet Fourteen

Writing for Elementary School Students

1. To become a better writer, work on your ability to visualize and describe concrete objects, action pictures, and scenes in a book.

2. Another exercise is to pick two objects, describe them, and then discuss how each is similar and different. As you get better at this, you will be able to increase the number and complexity of what is the same or different.

3. When you are ready to practice writing a paragraph, use Worksheets Six and Seven with the umbrella pictures. The top of the umbrella is used as the main idea, the topic sentence that holds the umbrella together. The sections that support the top piece are the areas for supporting information, evidence, and explanations. To beautify the umbrella, you add fringes that are like the descriptive details of your paragraph. Finally, the concluding sentence is like the handle on the umbrella, because it ties everything above it together.

4. When you are ready to write an essay, try using these techniques to help you get started. Remember that there is a great deal of organization, both in your mind and on paper, that must happen before writing a great essay.
    a. Ask questions
    b. CLOZE activity
    c. Brainstorm
    d. Mind map

Strategy Six, Worksheet Fifteen

Writing for Middle School Students

1. To become a better writer, work on your ability to visualize and describe concrete objects, action pictures, and scenes in a book.

2. Another exercise is to pick two objects, describe them, and then discuss how each is similar and different. As you get better at this, you will be able to increase the number and complexity of what is the same or different.

3. Practice writing excellent paragraphs by using Worksheets Five and Six with the umbrella pictures. The top of the umbrella is used as the main idea, the topic sentence that holds the umbrella together. The sections that support the top piece are the areas for supporting information, evidence, and explanations. To beautify the umbrella, you add fringes that are like the descriptive details of your paragraph. Finally, the concluding sentence is like the handle on the umbrella, because it ties everything above it together.

4. Ready to write an essay? Get organized before writing by using an outline or mind maps and the S.E.E. method. Be sure each paragraph has an introductory sentence (a main idea) followed by supporting details. Remember, you can begin writing with the body paragraphs and write the introduction and conclusion last.

5. Once the essay is written, check each paragraph to be sure it supports the central thesis and logically transitions into the next paragraph.

6. Next, read it, re-read it, and edit as necessary. Pay special attention to spelling and punctuation.

7. Use the buddy system to have a friend, teacher, and/or parent review the essay to make sure there are no glaring errors.

Strategy Six, Worksheet Sixteen

Writing for High School Students

1. What happens when you have difficulty writing your thesis statement? First, ask yourself what you are trying to prove. Write down all the ideas that occur to you and then begin crossing out the ones that are not applicable to your subject matter. Then look at all the ideas and try to condense them into two sentences, one if your teacher requires just a one-sentence thesis.

2. Get organized before writing. Using the umbrella technique, mind maps, or your favorite outline, always plan out your ideas before writing.

3. Write the body of the essay using the S.E.E. method (Statement, Evidence or Example, Explanation). Be sure each paragraph has an introductory sentence (a main idea) followed by supporting details.

4. Write the introduction using the funnel method of beginning with a broad overview of the theme to be discussed, then narrowing the theme to a more specific topic, and finally, writing the thesis statement.

5. Write the conclusion by summarizing the main ideas of the essay and developing a "So What?"

6. Check each paragraph to be sure it supports the central thesis and logically transitions into the next paragraph.

7. After the essay is completed, read it, re-read it, and edit as necessary. Pay special attention to spelling and punctuation.

8. Use the buddy system to have a friend, teacher, and/or parent review the essay to make sure there are no glaring errors.

Strategy Six, Worksheet Seventeen

Final Check

Title

- Is centered and capitalized correctly
- Uses clear and descriptive language

Each sentence

- Has a varied beginning
- Contains a subject and verb and expresses a complete thought

Each paragraph

- Begins with a topic sentence that is an overview of the paragraph. Be sure the topic sentence relates back to the thesis.
- Contains evidence that supports the topic sentence
- Explains how the evidence supports the topic sentence
- Ends with a transition to the next paragraph.

Wording

- Uses adjectives and adverbs to create vivid images
- Uses action verbs instead of just "telling" verbs

Writing Mechanics: Punctuation, Spelling, and Capitalization

- Each sentence begins with a capital letter and ends with appropriate punctuation.
- All proper nouns are capitalized.
- Check that commas and semi-colons are used correctly.
- Watch out for apostrophes in possessive words.
- Spelling is correct throughout. If you're using a computer, be extra careful to check the spelling of words. Remember that words such as "their," "there," and "they're" may not be distinguished by the computer.

Strategy Six, Worksheet Eighteen

Homework

A user removable worksheet is available on page 189 of the user worksheet section.

There is no specific homework for this strategy, because school life itself presents several opportunities for practicing effective writing skills. Although your child may not be formally writing every day, reward her in the "Writing" section of the Reward Chart each time she does one of the following:

- Uses a pre-writing strategy, such as visualization, brainstorming, asking questions, a CLOZE activity, or a mind map.

- Writes an effective introduction or conclusion.

- Writes a paragraph or an essay using either the Umbrella or S.E.E. writing structure.

- Remembers the "Final Check" to catch mechanical writing errors and unclear transitions.

- Prepares for essay questions on a test by brainstorming, determining main ideas and supporting details, and using a sample organizer.

- Correctly completes one of the steps for writing a research paper:
  - Set a schedule.
  - Choose a topic.
  - Research.
  - Take notes.
  - Develop a thesis.
  - Outline.
  - Write.
  - Edit and revise.

Strategy Six, Worksheet Eighteen

Reward Chart

A user removable worksheet is available on page 191 of the user worksheet section.

		Monday	Tuesday	Wednesday	Thursday	Friday	Saturday	Sunday
Assignment Notebook	Color coding							
	"Don't Forget" section							
	Writing something in every subject							
	Check/cross check							
Binder	Papers filed							
	Pockets used							
Other	Daily check in/out							
Time Management	Time log							
	Guess/actual time sheets							
	Wearing a watch							
	Using a monthly calendar							
Studying Strategies	Actively Reading							
	New Study Strategy							
	New Study Strategy							
Memory	Memory Strategy							
	Memory Strategy							
	Memory Strategy							
Note-Taking	Practices taking notes							
Writing	Uses a pre-writing strategy							
	Practices S.E.E.							

Strategy Six

BEFORE MOVING ON . . .

You're Done!
But are you ever really done?

Imagine a mother who hires a professional organizer to arrange her closet. Does this mean she will never have to hang clothes or put away shoes again? Of course not!

In the same way, organizational systems that you have put into place for your student will need constant monitoring and attention to stay effective. As the student becomes more proficient in using the *Thinking Organized*™ strategies, he will need your help less and less. However, depending on the age, motivation, and developmental level of your child, you may need to continue daily or weekly checks well into high school.

In teaching and practicing effective executive functioning skills with your student, you have given him an invaluable gift—the ability to manage his time and materials, study, learn and memorize information, gain knowledge from reading, and communicate effectively in writing. Not only will your student ultimately do better in school because of these newly acquired skills, but his facility for planning and negotiating daily life will also improve. You have given your child the skills necessary to succeed in school, life, and in whatever career awaits him in the years ahead. *Congratulations!*

LET US KNOW!

The *Thinking Organized*™ program has been refined by years of working with students, and it is continually improving. If you have a suggestion or a question for *Thinking Organized*™, please contact us through our website, www.thinkingorganized.com or by e-mail at info@thinkingorganized.com.

Glossary

acronym: A word formed from the initial letters of a series of words. Example: SUV = Sport Utility Vehicle.

acrostic: A series of words in which the first letter from each word forms a name, motto, or message when read in sequence. Example: ROY G. BIV stands for the colors of the rainbow—red, orange, yellow, green, blue, indigo, and violet

active working memory: Where information is temporarily held and manipulated while completing tasks such as listening, comprehending, or formulating a response.

assignment notebook: A central source where all assignments and responsibilities are recorded.

Attention Deficit Disorder/Attention Deficit Hyperactivity Disorder: A neurological disorder characterized by lack of impulse control, forgetfulness, an inability to concentrate, and/or hyperactivity.

auditory learning style: The preference to learn by hearing or speaking.

chunking: Dividing information into smaller, similar segments.

CLOZE activities: A method of beginning the writing process by developing key sentences with a word or phrase left blank.

conclusion: The end of an essay or research paper in which the student reiterates the thesis of the paper and suggests meaningful implications.

Cornell Outlining System: A system of taking notes in which the main idea is written on the left side of a page, supporting details or pictures are listed on the right, and a one-sentence summary is written at the bottom. Detailed in Walter Pauk's *How to Study in College for Cornell.*

Executive Function: The mental organizational process where one can plan and sequence ideas or activities and then implement, monitor, and revise those activities as needed.

Executive Function Weaknesses: When an individual experiences difficulties initiating, planning, organizing, and completing work. Frequently involves problems with attention, awareness of time, working memory, and cognitive flexibility.

kinesthetic learning style: A preference to learn by moving, doing, and touching.

language processing: The ability to process and understand verbal or written language.

loci: Mapping a mental pathway of familiar places in order to facilitate memory.

long-term memory: Where information is securely stored in memory and can be retrieved as needed.

material organization: The ability to properly catalog and maintain one's physical possessions.

memory strategies: Skills to help improve one's ability to remember.

mind map: A method of using pictures to demonstrate how ideas and facts relate to each other.

note-taking: The process of gathering the main or important ideas from a selection of text and writing them in a brief format to study later.

S.E.E.: A method of organized writing in which the student makes a Statement about what is going to be explained; gives Evidence from general knowledge, text material, or research; and Explains how the evidence supports the statement

short-term memory: Where information is stored temporarily by using memory strategies such as mnemonic devices or repetition. The information is not retained unless put into long-term memory.

time management: An ability to be aware of the passage of time and to structure time effectively in order to accomplish daily tasks

Two-Column note-taking system: A system of taking notes in which the student writes a main idea on the left column and supporting details on the right.

umbrella: A method of explaining organized writing in which the top is the main idea, each panel is a supporting idea, the metal supports are explanations and details, and the handle ties it all together (conclusion).

visual learning style: The preference for learning by seeing or reading. The most common learning style.

visualization: The process of mentally picturing an image, item, or words.

Bibliography

Bell, Nanci. *Visualizing and Verbalizing for Language Comprehension and Thinking*. San Luis Obispo: Gander Educational Publishing, 1986.

Brown, Ph.D., Thomas E. *Attention-Deficit Disorders and Comorbidities in Children, Adolescents, and Adults*. Washington, DC: American Psychiatric Press Inc., 2000.

Dawson, Peg and Richard Guare. *Executive Skills in Children and Adolescents: A Practical Guide to Assessment and Intervention*. New York: The Guilford Press, 2004.

Frender, Gloria. *Learning to Learn*. Nashville: Incentive Publication, Inc., 1990.

Goldberg, Mel Elkhonon. *The Executive Brain Frontal Lobes and the Civilized Mind*. New York: Oxford University Press, 2001.

Keeley, Susanne Phillips. *The Source for Executive Function Disorders*. East Moline, IL: LinguiSystems, Inc., 2003.

Levine, Mel. *Educational Care*. Cambridge: Educators Publishing Services, Inc.,1994.

Levine, Mel. *The Myth of Laziness*. New York: Simon and Schuster, 2003.

Luria, Aleksandr Romanovich. *Working Brain: An Introduction to Neuropsychology*. Harmondsworth, UK: Penguin Books Ltd., 1973.

Lyon, G. Reid and Norman A. *Krasnegor. Attention, Memory and Executive Function*. Baltimore: Paul H. Brookes Publishing Co., 1996.

Pauk, Walter. *How to Study in College*. (2nd ed). Boston. Houghton Mifflin Co., 1974.

Richard, Gail J. and Jill K. Fahy. *The Source for Development of Executive Functions*. East Moline, IL: LinguiSystems, Inc., 2005.

Richard, Gail J. and Joy L. Russell. *The Source for ADD/ADHD*. East Moline, IL: LinguiSystems, Inc., 2001.

Richards, Regina G. *The Source for Learning & Memory Strategies*. East Moline, IL: LinguiSystems, Inc., 2003.

About the Author

*R*hona M. Gordon, MS, CCC/SLP is an ASHA-certified speech and language pathologist and an organizational specialist with over thirty years of experience. In addition to working directly with parents, students, and therapists, she has served as a consultant to public and private schools in the Washington and New York metropolitan areas. Rhona provides training, both individualized and in group seminars, to parents and school administrators on effective organizational strategies that can be used in the home or classroom. She also trains executives and associations on office organization to achieve a smoother workflow. Rhona is a frequent contributor to parenting magazines and newsletters and a presenter at industry conferences. Her affiliations include:

- American Speech and Hearing Association (ASHA)
- Maryland State Speech and Hearing Association
- Washington Independent Services for Educational Resources (WISER)

Rhona is a dynamic speaker with a great sense of humor and enthusiastic personality that reassures parents and motivates students. For more information about Rhona Gordon and to bring her to your group, organization or school visit www.thinkingorganized.com.

Worksheets

User
Removable
Worksheets

Strategy One, User Worksheet One

Subject	Monday __/__	Tuesday __/__	Wednesday __/__	Thursday __/__	Friday __/__	Saturday __/__	Sunday __/__
_____	☐	☐	☐	☐	☐	☐	☐
_____	☐	☐	☐	☐	☐	☐	☐
_____	☐	☐	☐	☐	☐	☐	☐
_____	☐	☐	☐	☐	☐	☐	☐
_____	☐	☐	☐	☐	☐	☐	☐
_____	☐	☐	☐	☐	☐	☐	☐
Don't Forget							
Extra Curricular							
Teacher's Signature							
Parent's Signature							

Join us at **ThinkingOrganized.com**

Strategy One, User Worksheet Three

Assignment Notebook Rules

Tape this page to the inside of the assignment notebook.

1. Create a "Don't Forget" section for each week when you label your subjects for the month.

2. Color code all information:
     Red = Test or Quiz
     Blue = Long-term Project
     Black = Nightly Homework
     Green = Fun

3. Complete every box every day.
     If there is no homework, write "NONE" in the box.

4. Make a section for extracurricular activities, including tutoring, sports, clubs, or religious school.

5. Create and use a check/cross-check box.
     ☑ Check when assignment is completed.
     ☒ Cross-check when assignment is packed in binder.

Ask Mom or Dad to sign the assignment notebook every night.
He or she can only sign when Steps 1–5 have been completed.

Join us at **ThinkingOrganized.com**

Strategy One, User Worksheet Four

Maintain a properly organized assignment notebook and binder system. Remember to use the check in/check out location when arriving or leaving home. Points can be awarded for each day that the systems are used correctly.

Reward Chart

		Monday	Tuesday	Wednesday	Thursday	Friday	Saturday	Sunday
Assignment Notebook	Color coding							
	"Don't Forget" section							
	Writing something in every subject							
Binder	Check/cross check							
	Papers filed							
Other	Pockets used							

Strategy One, User Worksheet Four

Maintain a properly organized assignment notebook and binder system. Remember to use the check in/check out location when arriving or leaving home. Points can be awarded for each day that the systems are used correctly.

Reward Chart

		Monday	Tuesday	Wednesday	Thursday	Friday	Saturday	Sunday
Assignment Notebook	Color coding							
	"Don't Forget" section							
	Writing something in every subject							
Binder	Check/cross check							
	Papers filed							
Other	Pockets used							

Strategy Two, Worksheet Two

How Do I Spend My Time? Week of ___/___/___ to ___/___/___

Time	Monday __/__	Tuesday __/__	Wednesday __/__	Thursday __/__	Friday __/__	Saturday __/__	Sunday __/__
7:00 AM							
8:00 AM							
9:00 AM							
10:00 AM							
11:00 AM							
12:00 PM							
1:00 PM							
2:00 PM							
3:00 PM							
4:00 PM							
5:00 PM							
6:00 PM							
7:00 PM							
8:00 PM							
9:00 PM							
10:00 PM							
11:00 PM							
12:00 AM							

Join us at **ThinkingOrganized.com**

Strategy Two, Worksheet Two

How Do I Spend My Time? Week of ___/___/___ to ___/___/___

Time	Monday _/_	Tuesday _/_	Wednesday _/_	Thursday _/_	Friday _/_	Saturday _/_	Sunday _/_
7:00 AM							
8:00 AM							
9:00 AM							
10:00 AM							
11:00 AM							
12:00 PM							
1:00 PM							
2:00 PM							
3:00 PM							
4:00 PM							
5:00 PM							
6:00 PM							
7:00 PM							
8:00 PM							
9:00 PM							
10:00 PM							
11:00 PM							
12:00 AM							

Join us at **ThinkingOrganized.com**

Strategy Two, Worksheet Two

How Do I Spend My Time? Week of ___/___/___ to ___/___/___

Blank Time Log

Time	Monday __/__	Tuesday __/__	Wednesday __/__	Thursday __/__	Friday __/__	Saturday __/__	Sunday __/__
7:00 AM							
8:00 AM							
9:00 AM							
10:00 AM							
11:00 AM							
12:00 PM							
1:00 PM							
2:00 PM							
3:00 PM							
4:00 PM							
5:00 PM							
6:00 PM							
7:00 PM							
8:00 PM							
9:00 PM							
10:00 PM							
11:00 PM							
12:00 AM							

Join us at **ThinkingOrganized.com**

Strategy Two, Worksheet Five

Guess/Actual Time Sheet

Prioritize	Homework/Activity	Guess Time to Complete	Actual Time to Complete

NOTES:

Join us at **ThinkingOrganized.com**

Strategy Two, Worksheet Five

Guess/Actual Time Sheet

Prioritize	Homework/Activity	Guess Time to Complete	Actual Time to Complete

NOTES:

Strategy Two, Worksheet Five

Guess/Actual Time Sheet

Prioritize	Homework/Activity	Guess Time to Complete	Actual Time to Complete

NOTES:

Join us at **ThinkingOrganized.com**

Strategy Two, Worksheet Five

Guess/Actual Time Sheet

Prioritize	Homework/Activity	Guess Time to Complete	Actual Time to Complete

NOTES:

Join us at **ThinkingOrganized.com**

Strategy Two, Worksheet Ten

Blank Monthly Calendar

RED = Tests or quizzes • BLUE = Long-term projects • BLACK = Nightly homework, however if you are using an assignment notebook it is not necessary to put homework on the long-term calendar • GREEN = Fun activities or weekly obligations

Sunday	Monday	Tuesday	Wednesday	Thursday	Friday	Saturday

Strategy Two, Worksheet Ten

Blank Monthly Calendar

RED = Tests or quizzes • BLUE = Long-term projects • BLACK = Nightly homework, however if you are using an assignment notebook it is not necessary to put homework on the long-term calendar • GREEN = Fun activities or weekly obligations

Sunday	Monday	Tuesday	Wednesday	Thursday	Friday	Saturday

Strategy Two, Worksheet Eleven

Homework

Throughout this week, help your child practice estimating, recording, and noticing time by using the time logs, guess/actual time sheets, the monthly calendar, and her watch. Remember to continue to give points for use of the assignment notebook and binder as introduced in Strategy One.

Reward Chart

		Monday	Tuesday	Wednesday	Thursday	Friday	Saturday	Sunday
Assignment Notebook	Color coding							
	"Don't Forget" section							
	Writing something in every subject							
	Check/cross check							
Binder	Papers filed							
	Pockets used							
Other	Daily check in/out							
Time Management	Time log							
	Guess/ actual time sheets							
	Wearing a watch							

Join us at **ThinkingOrganized.com**

Strategy Three, Worksheet One

Learning Styles Assessment Questionnaire

Read each question carefully with your child and then decide together which answer best describes him.

Questions	One	Two	Three
When learning something new in science, do you prefer to:	read the textbook	listen to an explanation	complete an experiment in the science lab
When studying for a spelling test, do you:	try to picture the word in your mind	recite the letters out loud or in your head	write the word to see if it "feels" right
Do you prefer stories with:	good descriptions, so you can picture the scene	good dialogue, so you can understand what is happening between the characters	lots of action, because it is hard to sit still and read
How do you stay focused when listening to a long lecture?	take notes	take no notes but listen closely	take sporadic notes, even if you choose not to use them later
If you are trying to concentrate, do you get distracted by:	clutter or movement nearby	sounds and noises, either too quiet or too loud	activity happening around you
If packing gear for a soccer game (or any extracurricular activity) do you:	make a list in your head or on paper	wait for your mother to call out what you need	just start packing without thinking about it first
When you have a problem, do you:	organize your thoughts with lists	talk to yourself or a friend	engage in a physical activity, like walking around or jogging
When talking to a friend, do you:	like to meet the person face-to-face	prefer to talk on the phone	walk or move around as you talk
If you run into someone you have only met once before, you are most likely to remember:	his face or how he looked	his name or the sound of his voice	his mannerisms or hand motions

INTERPRET YOUR RESULTS!

If most of the responses are ones, your student seems to prefer a visual approach to learning.

If most of the responses are twos, your student seems to prefer an auditory approach to learning.

If most of the responses are threes, your student seems to prefer a kinesthetic approach to learning.

Strategy Three, Worksheet Three

Studying for a Test, Part One

ON YOUR MARK . . .

Start with Good Studying Habits

1. To really make studying easy, *review your class notes on a weekly basis*. All you have to do is read them over at the end of the week and clarify any confusing information. This ten-minute exercise will help you become familiar with the material and make studying for the test much easier.

2. *Start studying for a test five days in advance and for a quiz, three days.*

3. *Schedule your studying time* on your daily calendar and write down what you will study each night. It is not good enough to write the word "study" in your assignment notebook. Divide your material into manageable parts so that you will have a specific amount of material to cover each night. Plan to finish studying all the material at least two days before the test, so that the night before the test can be devoted to difficult areas and a general review.

4. *Collect all of your information* from class notes, worksheets, textbook, quizzes, and previous tests. If your notes are not complete or legible, copy them from a friend or ask the teacher if you can borrow his notes. When you start far enough ahead of time to prepare for an exam, you have the time to see what is missing or incomplete. Then you have a chance to remedy the situation. Remember, if you only have 70 percent of the information to study, you can only answer 70 percent of the questions!

5. *Create a comprehensive study guide.* Use your class outline or an outline from the textbook as your basis. Then add information from other sources to make a comprehensive outline. As you add information, you are already studying and putting small chunks of information systematically in your brain. This makes retrieval of information much easier. If you are a kinesthetic or auditory learner, talk out loud to anyone who will listen or to yourself as you put all of your information onto one outline. Add additional information in different colors. For example, if you add to your class notes, use green to signify that material is being added from the textbook and use blue to show information added from handouts. This allows you to refer back to the source if there is a question you want to clarify.

You will know about 80 percent of the material when you have finished creating the comprehensive study guide!

Join us at **ThinkingOrganized.com**

Strategy Three, Worksheet Four

Studying for a Test, Part Two

GET SET . . .

Specific Techniques for Learning the Remaining 20 Percent.

You're on the Home Stretch!

- *Memory strategies* such as visualization, chunking, mnemonics, linking, rhyming, rhythms, and loci will help you remember facts, even under stress. Refer to Strategy Four for specific memory techniques. Rehearse and practice a lot.

- *Flash cards* can be a great studying tool for key terms and vocabulary. If you choose to use note cards, go through the cards daily. The cards that you do not know should be put in a separate pile and reviewed right before you fall asleep and first thing in the morning. These extra few minutes spent reviewing makes memorizing easier.

  Some kids use flash cards for everything. However, if you have a tendency to lose the cards, put the key terms and vocabulary on a sheet of paper. Divide the paper in half using the left side for the term and the right side for the definition.

- *Mind Maps* can help you interact with material to be learned by drawing pictures that represent written information. You can use visual images to help remember the order of events in a historical sequence or for organizing your thoughts on the main idea and details of the material being learned.

- *Timelines* can help you remember dates. Practice writing the dates on a timeline and then go back and fill in the important information about each date. Then explain *why* each date is important.

Join us at **ThinkingOrganized.com**

Strategy Three, Worksheet Five

Studying for a Test, Part Three

GO!

More Studying Strategies:

- **Form a study group.** In middle school and high school, it is often a good idea to study with others. Although some parents feel that actual work does not take place, study groups offer the opportunity to make sure each student understands the material and has studied in a comprehensive manner. Use the study session to quiz each other on important information and create outlines for possible essay questions. Reward yourself with a pizza or ice cream party *after* the studying is done.

- **Integrate the information.** This may be the hardest task of all. You have to ask yourself why the information is important and how one piece relates to another. Discuss this with other students, especially if you have a hard time understanding the main points and how they relate to the topic you are studying.

- **Prepare for an essay question.** For an essay question, you should prepare to write about *three to five* points about a subject area. Write down how each point you will make relates to the main topic. Provide an example from the material to support each statement.

- **Questions?** Have a sheet ready to jot down questions that you can ask your teacher or a classmate at least two days before the exam. If you keep the sheet with you as you begin studying, your questions will be ready for the teacher. Also, as you become more familiar with the material, you may answer your own questions.

- **The night before** the exam should be for a general review and to go over the more difficult pieces of the material.

- **Any information** that continues to be difficult to memorize should be reviewed once before you go to sleep and then again on the way to the test.

You are ready and well prepared for your test!
Good Luck!

Join us at **ThinkingOrganized.com**

Strategy Three, Worksheet Six

Remember to Do the Following When Memorizing Material

1. Start to memorize material as *soon* as you get it. Remember, memorization takes a lot of repetition.

2. Read the material carefully, to yourself. Are there any pictures you can put in your mind about what you have just read?

3. Repeat the information out loud *a lot*.

4. Use memorization strategies like visualization, chunking, mnemonics, linking, rhyming, rhythms, and loci. Look for patterns and if you get stuck, try to relate the hard pieces to things that are very familiar to you.

5. Write out the stanza or material you are trying to memorize. Any mistakes should be marked with a very bright color.

6. Repeat and write it again.

7. Now it's time to start cramming. The last two days before the test go over the material as much as possible.

8. The day before the test, review in the afternoon and again before you go to *bed*.

9. On the day of the test, review first thing in the morning and just before your class.

Strategy Three, Worksheet Seven

Use a variety of the studying techniques listed on the worksheets in this Strategy. Reward *each* method used separately to reinforce the value of trying more than one way to interact with material to be learned. Points are also awarded for active reading strategies such as note-taking or highlighting.

Reward Chart

		Monday	Tuesday	Wednesday	Thursday	Friday	Saturday	Sunday
Assignment Notebook	Color coding							
	"Don't Forget" section							
	Writing something in every subject							
	Check/cross check							
Binder	Papers filed							
	Pockets used							
Other	Daily check in/out							
	Time log							
Time Management	Guess/actual time sheets							
	Wearing a watch							
	Using a monthly calendar							
Studying Strategies	Actively reading							
	New Study Strategy							
	New Study Strategy							

Join us at **ThinkingOrganized.com**

Strategy Four, Worksheet Six

Homework

Choose a memory challenge and use at least two of the strategies (visualization, chunking, acronyms, acrostics, rhyme and rhythm, loci, and combination) to memorize the information. Here are some ideas for your student's memory challenge:

- U.S. states (One memory challenge could include seven to ten states, such as the Southeast)

- Regional states and capitals

- Five Great Lakes

- List of foreign words

- List of vocabulary words

- Names of all your classmates (name all the girls or all the boys)

- Names of all the neighbors on your street

- Your family genealogy: list the names of your family members, aunts, uncles, cousins, and grandparents

- A section of the Periodic Table of Elements

- Grocery list (make up your own)

Join us at **ThinkingOrganized.com**

Strategy Four, Worksheet Six

		Monday	Tuesday	Wednesday	Thursday	Friday	Saturday	Sunday
Assignment Notebook	Color coding							
	"Don't Forget" section							
	Writing something in every subject							
	Check/cross check							
Binder	Papers filed							
	Pockets used							
Other	Daily check in/out							
Time Management	Time log							
	Guess/actual time sheets							
	Wearing a watch							
	Using a monthly calendar							
Studying Strategies	Actively reading							
	New Study Strategy							
	New Study Strategy							
Memory	Memory Strategy							
	Memory Strategy							
	Memory Strategy							

Join us at **ThinkingOrganized.com**

Strategy Five, Worksheet One

Main Idea	Details						

Strategy Five, Worksheet One

Blank Two-Column Note-taking Sheet

Main Idea	Details

Strategy Five, Worksheet One

Main Idea	Details

Strategy Five, Worksheet One

Blank Two-Column Note-taking Sheet

Main Idea	Details

Strategy Five, Worksheet Two

Image One to Practice Two-Column Note-taking System

Main Idea	Details

Strategy Five, Worksheet Four

Image Two to Practice Two-Column Note-Taking

Main Idea	Details

Strategy Five, Worksheet Six

Image Three to Practice Two-Column Note-Taking

Main Idea	Details

Strategy Five, Worksheet Eight

Image Four to Practice Two-Column Note-Taking

Main Idea	Details

Strategy Five, Worksheet Ten

Image Five to Practice Two-Column Note-Taking

Main Idea	Details

Strategy Five, Worksheet Twelve

Image Six to Practice Two-Column Note-Taking

Main Idea	Details

Strategy Five, Worksheet Fourteen

Image Seven to Practice Two-Column Note-Taking

Main Idea	Details

Join us at **ThinkingOrganized.com**

Strategy Five, Worksheet Sixteen

Cornell Outlining System

Key Phrase or Word	Main Idea	Supporting Idea
		Supporting Idea
		Detail
		Detail
		Supporting Idea
		Detail
		Detail
		Short Summary:

Strategy Five, Worksheet Sixteen

Cornell Outlining System

Key Phrase or Word	Main Idea	Supporting Idea
		Detail
		Detail
		Supporting Idea
		Detail
		Detail
		Short Summary:

Strategy Five, Worksheet Sixteen

Key Phrase or Word	Main Idea	Supporting Idea	
			Detail
			Detail
		Supporting Idea	
			Detail
			Detail
		Short Summary:	

Strategy Five, Worksheet Sixteen

Cornell Outlining System

Key Phrase or Word	Main Idea	Supporting Idea
		Detail
		Detail
	Supporting Idea	Detail
		Detail
	Short Summary:	

Strategy Five, Worksheet Twenty-Two

Have the student practice the Two-Column note-taking system or the Cornell Outlining System on an assignment from school or a social studies or science textbook chapter. See how much the student can do independently, but do not hesitate to help. Remember that it takes a great deal of practice and repetition before a student can take effective notes.

Reward Chart

		Monday	Tuesday	Wednesday	Thursday	Friday	Saturday	Sunday
Assignment Notebook	Color coding							
	"Don't Forget" section							
	Writing something in every subject							
	Check/cross check							
Binder	Papers filed							
	Pockets used							
Other	Daily check in/out							
Time Management	Time log							
	Guess/actual time sheets							
	Wearing a watch							
	Using a monthly calendar							
Studying Strategies	Actively reading							
	New Study Strategy							
	New Study Strategy							
Memory	Memory Strategy							
	Memory Strategy							
	Memory Strategy							
Note-Taking	Practice taking notes							

Strategy Five, Worksheet Twenty-Two

Have the student practice the Two-Column note-taking system or the Cornell Outlining System on an assignment from school or a social studies or science textbook chapter. See how much the student can do independently, but do not hesitate to help. Remember that it takes a great deal of practice and repetition before a student can take effective notes.

Reward Chart

		Monday	Tuesday	Wednesday	Thursday	Friday	Saturday	Sunday
Assignment Notebook	Color coding							
	"Don't Forget" section							
	Writing something in every subject							
	Check/cross check							
Binder	Papers filed							
	Pockets used							
Other	Daily check in/out							
	Time log							
Time Management	Guess/actual time sheets							
	Wearing a watch							
	Using a monthly calendar							
Studying Strategies	Actively reading							
	New Study Strategy							
	New Study Strategy							
Memory	Memory Strategy							
	Memory Strategy							
	Memory Strategy							
Note-Taking	Practice taking notes							

©2008, Rhona M. Gordon, Thinking Organized™. All Rights Reserved. Duplication permitted by owner of Thinking Organized for Parents and Children Workbook

Strategy Six, Worksheet One

Questions to Help You Get Started Writing Using the Sample Prompt,
"Video Games are Worthwhile"

What do you like about video games?

_____

_____

_____

What do you know about video games?

_____

_____

_____

Do video games involve any useful skills?

_____

_____

_____

Why are video games worthwhile?

_____

_____

_____

_____

Strategy Six, Worksheet Three

Practice CLOZE Activity

Three things I like about video games are _____ ,

_____ , and _____ . Two things that video games teach are

_____ and _____ .

My mother likes video games because _____ and _____

_____ . I also think video games are a good thing because _____

and _____ .

Strategy Six, Worksheet Eighteen

Homework

There is no specific homework for this strategy, because school life itself presents several opportunities for practicing effective writing skills. Although your child may not be formally writing every day, reward her in the "Writing" section of the Reward Chart each time she does one of the following:

- Uses a pre-writing strategy, such as visualization, brainstorming, asking questions, a CLOZE activity, or a mind map.

- Writes an effective introduction or conclusion.

- Writes a paragraph or an essay using either the Umbrella or S.E.E. writing structure.

- Remembers the "Final Check" to catch mechanical writing errors and unclear transitions.

- Prepares for essay questions on a test by brainstorming, determining main ideas and supporting details, and using a sample organizer.

- Correctly completes one of the steps for writing a research paper:
  - Set a schedule.
  - Choose a topic.
  - Research.
  - Take notes.
  - Develop a thesis.
  - Outline.
  - Write.
  - Edit and revise.

Join us at **ThinkingOrganized.com**

Strategy Six, Worksheet Eighteen

Reward Chart

		Monday	Tuesday	Wednesday	Thursday	Friday	Saturday	Sunday
Assignment Notebook	Color coding							
	"Don't Forget" section							
	Writing something in every subject							
	Check/cross check							
Binder	Papers filed							
	Pockets used							
Other	Daily check in/out							
	Time log							
Time Management	Guess/actual time sheets							
	Wearing a watch							
	Using a monthly calendar							
Studying Strategies	Actively Reading							
	New Study Strategy							
	New Study Strategy							
Memory	Memory Strategy							
	Memory Strategy							
	Memory Strategy							
Note-Taking	Practices taking notes							
Writing	Uses a pre-writing strategy							
	Practices S.E.E.							

Join us at **ThinkingOrganized**.com